French Kisses

by

George East

Illustrations by Robin Evans

Telephone: 023 92 678148
Facsimile: 023 92 665070
e-mail: info@la-puce.co.uk
website: www.la-puce.co.uk

© George East 2003

This paperback edition 2003

ISBN 0 9523635 7 7

The author asserts the moral right to
be identified as the author of this work

Designed and typeset by Nigel at Christianson Hoper Norman
Reprographics by SP Digital
Printed in Great Britain by Borcombe Printers PLC, Hampshire

Books by George East in the Mill of the Flea series:

Home & Dry in France
(A Year in Purgatory)

René & Me
(A Year with the Normandy Fox)

French Letters

French Flea Bites

French Cricket

French Kisses

Also by the same author:

A Year behind Bars
(The Publican's Tale)

LA PUCE PUBLICATIONS (UK)
87 Laburnum Grove, Portsmouth PO2 OHG
Telephone: 023 92 678148 Facsimile: 023 92 665070
e-mail: info@la-puce.co.uk
Website: www.la-puce.co.uk

Acknowledgement

It is customary for an author to dedicate a new book to someone because of his or her inspirational help with the creative process. I have generally tried to avoid this practice for fear of offending those people who think they are more deserving of a credit than the muse I have chosen. More often, I have avoided the practice for fear of crediting and thus offending people who would not want to be remotely associated with me or my books. This time and after much inner torment, I have decided to go for it and try and thank everyone who has in any way played any part in our small adventures in Lower Normandy across the years. It also allows me to write the longest sentence in literary history. If you are on this list, you will know why. If you are not and wanted to be, I am sorry. If you are and did not want to be included, rest assured I am thinking about someone else with the same name. I would like to buy you a drink, but this is a much cheaper way of showing my appreciation and even easier to organise. You, of course, are very welcome to buy me a drink when next we meet.

Here goes then, and my very sincere thanks to everyone who has been a Friend of the Flea across the years, but especially to André, Antoine, Adrian, Ace, Adrienne, Aristide, Anthony, Antony, Adam, Anthea, Aurora, Alistair, Alisdair, Alain, Alan, Albert, Alison, Alex, Angela, Amie, Anne-Marie, Amelie, Anne, Ann, Andrew, Bryan, Brian, Bernie, Bernice, Bob, Bernard, Brett, Barry, Blanche, Budgie, Brenda, Bill, Big Albie, Barbara, Bertrand, Ben, Brigitte, Bridget, Coco, Catherine, Cato, Con, Cyril, Charlie, Carl, Clare, Clair, Campbell, Clin, Carol, Carole, Cormac, Crystal, Cathy, Charles, Cuba, Chris, Christianne, Chantal, Colin, Collette, Claudette, Christine, Charlotte, Cherry, Cilla, Corinne, Cheryl, Claude, Didier, Daisy, Darren, Desmond, Dominic, Dominique, Daniel, Dawn, David, Don, Debbie, Donna, Dot, Duncan, Doug, Dickie, Derek, Daphne, Eugene, Eddie, Emily, Emile, Emma, Eduoard, Ellen, Elizabeth, Eve, Ermintrude, Eric, Enid, Elaine, Francoise, Francois, Fran, Freddo, Felix, Fred, Frazer, Freda,

Frank, Fay, Faye, Fenella, Fiona, George, Georges, Graham, Guy, Gemma, Greg, Gerard, Gerald, Guilliame, Gert, Grant, Gilly, Garry, Gary, Ghislaine, Gilbert, Geoff, Gladstone, Gladys, Harvey, Hector, Heinz, Hilary, Harry, Hen, Honor, Hattie, Hannah, Hazel, Helen, Helena, Heather, Holly, Havana, Harold, Howard, Hugh, Herbert, Henri, Hubert, Ian, Iris, Innes, Irene, John, Jimmy, Julian, Jeanne, Jack, Janet, Jon, Jackie, Jacqui, Joy, July, Judy, Julie, Julia, Jeff, Janetta, James, Jane, Jacques, Janine, Jacko, Jean, Jodie, Jean-Marie, Jean-Claude, Jean-Jacques, JayPay, Joan, Joanne, Josephine, Jenny, June, Jocyline, Jocelyn, Kurt, Keno, Kath, Kari, Kara, Kathy, Katie, Kathleen, Keith, Ken, Kris, Karin, Karen, Kim, Kelly, Kevin, Lucky, Lucy, Lorraine, Labeeb, Louise, Louis, Linda, Libby, Luc, Laurence, Lilly, Laura, Lara, Lili, Les, Len, Lynn, Mark, Miguel, Milly, Mo-Mo, Mad, Maggie, Marie, Musky, Mary, Matt, Matthew, Maire, Mel, Martine, Mavis, Mandy, Marine, Maureen, Mickey, Molly, Michael, Maurice, Morrie, Michel, Michelle, Marcel, Margaret, Nigel, Norah, Norman, Nan, Nini, Neil, Neville, Naomi, Olwen, Olga, Oliver, Oscar, Old Pierrot, Penny, Pyscho, Pierre, Pee-Wee, Phylis, Phillipe, Percy, Peter, Patrick, Patrice, Pam, Pat, Paul, Paolo, Pauline, Queenie, René, Racine, Ray, Regis, Roger, Ronnie, Rosie, Rab, Rachel, Reggie, Richard, Ralph, Robin, Rutger, Robert, Ross, Rob, Rolf, Sadie, Sadika, Solange, Sugar, Sarah, Sara, Suzie, Sue, Susan, Sharon, Serge, Sophie, Shep, Simon, Stuart, Stan, Sally, Shirley, Stephen, Sylvia, Steve, Sid, Sufie, Thierry, Trevor, Tom, Trish, Tim, Tosh, Terry, Terri, Thomas, Tony, Tina, Toots, Unwin, Vincent, Victor, Vanessa, Victoria, Vivian, Vivyan, Vera, Val, Valerie, William, Warren, Wilfred, Wally, Wolfie, Young Pierrot, Yves, Yvonne, Yvette, Zelda, Zoe, and finally, the ageless Madame Zizi.

Thanks for the memories, and hope to see you soon. When we do meet, by the way, mine's the usual very large *galopin* of Normandy champagne…

Part One

They spell it Vinci and pronounce it Vinchy;
foreigners always spell better than they pronounce.

The Innocents Abroad.

For me, just one of the delights of living in a foreign land is the chance to learn something new and interesting every day. It might be the discovery of a particularly subtle aspect of the culture in which we have chosen to live. It might be a small epiphany revealing how nurture will often triumph over human nature, or the reverse. Quite often, I find the revelation is the result of a simple linguistic cock-up. The final minutes in another year of our lives in Lower Normandy are ticking away, and in the past hour I have learned another important lesson in life: it is very difficult to play *Swannee River* on the spoons while dressed as a carrot.

We are gathered in the Flaming Curtains to see the new year in, and the bar is as full as a doctor's waiting-room when rumours of an interesting virus are sweeping through our extremely health-conscious community. While I attempt to wave my empty glass in the direction of our host Coco, I engage Morton the pub dog in conversation and explain that I am wearing a carrot suit because of yet another small but significant communications problem.

Even after many years of living in this quiet corner of Normandy, I still regularly fall victim to the idiosyncrasies of local usage. When Coco telephoned this morning to ask if I would be doing my usual party piece with the spoons and kazoo, I thought he said that all the other foreigners - by which he of course meant British settlers - would be wearing fancy dress. On arrival I realised he had meant formal dress, and

3

found myself a lonely giant vegetable amongst a monochrome forest of bow ties and black dresses. It says something about the local people's view of the British community that nobody has commented on the costume I shall be wearing at this year's Carrot Festival.

During our time in Lower Normandy I have often observed that most local people think all British settlers are rich and either harmlessly eccentric or completely barking mad. To be fair, they often have good reason for coming to that conclusion.

*   *   *   *   *

A little later, and despite the chill our group has moved on to the terrace. We are gathered at the rickety table which Coco calls the British Embassy. In her less generous moments, my wife calls it the overseas branch of Alcoholics Unanimous. At other times she says it should be known as King George's Round Table because it is where I most like to hold court. It is true that the table is a favourite meeting place for our informal club of settlers and locals, and that I like to talk. This, I often tell Donella, is why I am a writer. I think I have something to say and want people to listen. Besides and as in any half-decent pub, drinking and talking go naturally together.

As well as being a gathering place for debate and discourse, scandal and intrigue, our special table is also distinguished by the apple tree growing through its centre. According to legend, the tree sprang from the remains of an English Cox which a French farmer tried and then discarded after one tentative bite. Impressed by the tenacity and determination of the sapling and rather than going to the bother of rearranging the seating, Coco simply cut a hole in the table top. Although it has not born fruit in the decade I have been sitting beneath its branches, the tree is now a sturdy growth and if it could speak it would have some interesting tales to tell. Each year as the trunk gets bigger, Coco enlarges the hole, and how the table was so ingeniously fitted around the tree is an interesting conversation piece for breaking the ice with visitors.

The alleged history of how the tree came to be here is also a perfect example of why we choose to live in rural France. If the tale is true, the apple came from Britain, was initially treated with suspicion and ignored, but hung on, spread it roots and bided its time until it was accepted as part of the community.

As we sit and drink and think about the dying year and how it has treated us, an impish wind explores the high street and hurries yet more revellers towards the bar, which lies in the shadow of what is said to be the oldest church in Normandy (if not all France). This arrangement is most convenient as the people of the town still cling mostly to the old faith. Coco's wife Chantal also serves the best and cheapest food in the area, so nobody has far to travel to satisfy soul or stomach or both. Having such a broad church of clientele, the *Rideau Cramoisi* is also the official information exchange centre for the town and surrounding area, and the high proportion of British expatriates amongst the regular customers ensures there is always a juicy story about foreign and therefore bizarre activities to hear and pass on.

After a warning crackle and howl, the loudspeakers lining the high street blare into life and we decide unanimously to return to the crowded bar rather than sit through yet another replay of the town's favourite seasonal pop songs. Though accomplished in so many other areas of creativity, the French do not seem to have quite got the hang of most forms of modern music. The big hit this year in our area is a lament about a boy whose dog is run over on Christmas Eve as his mother lies dying of consumption. Other tunes and themes are even less life-affirming. As rock god Johnny Hallyday turns sixty next year there is also the danger of a tribute medley of his greatest hits, which will inevitably include the classic French language version of *Dah Doo Ron Ron.*

We squeeze into the bar just as the church clock strikes midnight, but know this is a false alarm. Like many of the townspeople and particularly the local craftsmen, the clock seems to run on its own time. Rival bar owners allege that our host at the Flaming Curtains has an arrangement with the verger so that the clock goes forward when Coco wants an early night or backwards when he scents a profitable session, but I know this is not true. Like all good Frenchmen, Coco Lecoq is a great believer in liberty over licence, and opens and shuts the bar regardless of the official hours of trading.

While fighting my way to the bar counter, I explore Donella's purse and see that our supply of old money should just last out the evening. This thought evokes a pang of nostalgia as it will be the last occasion in forty years that I shall be buying my drinks with French francs. Although the rest of France has been trading in euros for some time, Coco declared the Curtains an independent financial state on changeover day. On the eve of the death of the franc I found him feeding the fire in the public bar with a sheaf of official papers giving details of the precise and compulsory phasing-out of the old currency. When I asked him about his plans for a smooth transition he explained that, like Britain, he was waiting for more favourable conditions before officially adopting the euro. Apart from being another example of the sort of attitude that attracts us to life in this country, Coco's refusal to conform was also a shrewd business move as it allows local farmers to launder their hoards of undeclared and thus tax-free francs while enjoying a break from the demands of market day.

Waiting at the bar, I feel a friendly nudge, and turn to see that my friend Jean-Claude Goulot is out on the town, and that he is not wearing his trademark brown overalls. A defiantly individualistic personality even by rural Norman standards, Jean-Claude is acknowledged as the best producer of bootleg calvados apple brandy in the area and said to be a very competent carpenter in his spare time. Though I can vouch for the quality and strength of his *calva* I do not know much about his abilities at working with wood, as we have been waiting for him to fit a door in a hole in the mill cottage since he first gave us an estimate in 1994. Over the years he has become a good friend, and calls in at least once a week to see if the hole is still there.

When I ask how business is going, Jean-Claude says he is as busy as a bull in a field of cows but has decided to abandon the demands of carpentry to set out on a new career path. While I buy him a whisky he proudly takes out and shows me his new set of dentures, then announces that he has decided to become a leg of lamb. When he has put his teeth back and enlarges on his plans, I realise that he has decided on a lifestyle as a *gigolo* rather than a *gigot*. Although he is certainly small enough to qualify as a toy boy, he will never see sixty again and is also not handsome in the conventional sense, even for rural France. Whatever his qualifications, my friend is obviously dressed for his new role. Apart from the new teeth and a rather obvious wig, he is wearing platform-soled shoes and a suit which even the most extrovert character would have been embarrassed to wear at a small town 70's disco during a power cut. In a subtle shade of tangerine, it is at least two sizes too big and the ultra-flared trousers cascade onto the floor like a set of badly-made Austrian blinds.

After some adjustment of his dentures - which he seems to have put in upside down - Jean says the idea of his new business venture came about, somewhat predictably, after spending an evening in the bar with Didier Bouvier. It does not surprise me that our local entrepreneur and rogue trader lies behind the scheme, or that Jean bought his ill-fitting teeth, clothing (and other vital appliances, artifices and equipment not mentioned in polite company) from Dodgy Didier.

While I get Jean-Claude another drink, he explains the *raison d'être* behind his new enterprise. It is a fact, he says, that the local freesheet is always full of advertisements placed by single women in search of male company and even marriage. His big idea for the new year is to set up business as an escort agency with himself as resident *gigolo*, and split the profits with Didier. He also believes that he has got one over on Didier for a change, as he will have all the pleasure and Didier will only get half the money resulting from his assignations. Also, if he meets a rich widow, he will marry her and he will be able to retire. As a final and unarguable argument for the Cartesian logic of his business plan, my friend points out that the notorious Widow of Négreville is never short of customers. She is marginally less attractive than the rear end of a cow suffering from the runs and has a bigger moustache than most of her visitors. It is also surely time, he concludes, that the modern craze for gender equality reached our area.

Asked for my opinion of his New Year resolution, I settle for making vaguely approving noises and decide not to ask what Madame Goulot thinks about her husband selling his body rather than his carpentry skills.

While Jean-Claude is practising some of his conversational gambits on an elderly lady who has obviously turned her hearing-aid off, unpleasantness breaks out nearby as we come as close to a punch-up as I have seen in any French rural bar. Two elderly local farmers are toe-to-toe, and the situation is only resolved when Coco intervenes.

As the atmosphere returns to normal, I ask our host if he knows the source of the disagreement. Coco gives a modified version of the all-purpose gallic shrug then explains that the argument is, for once, not about a boundary dispute but stems from a confrontation at a recent meeting of the St. Sauveur hunting club. As the first fusillade of rifles, shotguns and other assorted weaponry rang out, the small farmer's male dog took advantage of the confusion and mounted the bitch belonging to the large farmer. Although this would normally cause little comment, when the owner of the randy dog refused to apologise for the incident, the owner of the bitch demanded a token fee of ten euros for the pleasure the animal had had. Outraged, the small farmer retorted that any payment should be the other way round as the female was known to be the ugliest dog in the area.

Having settled the disagreement by reminding the participants that their bar bills are due, Coco climbs on to the bar and calls the house to order. Anticipating an acknowledgement of our contributions to his retirement fund during the past months and an invitation to refill our glasses and toast the New Year in, the crowd presses forward eagerly. But gasps of disappointment mingle with the grunts of crowded discomfort when Coco's invitation to drink up is followed by the announcement that the Flaming Curtains is closing a full quarter of an hour before the New Year arrives.

As our host descends from the bar and makes for the door, mass shrugging breaks out as the customers discuss this development. To appreciate the scene, it is important to understand that the gallic shrug is infinitely more sophisticated in style and significance than its lacklustre British equivalent, which uses the shoulders to demonstrate no more than lack of knowledge or concern. In its kaleidoscopic variety of manifestations, the French shrug not only makes full use of shoulders, arms and hands, but also mouth, nose, eyes, eyebrows and even in extreme cases, ears. In a deft combination of twitches, jerks and spasms, the shrugger can convey an almost limitless range of emotions, concerns and comments to the shrugee. I have heard of meetings between accomplished French shruggers where the participants conversed happily for more than an hour without a word being spoken. There is even claimed to be a shruggers' convention held in Paris each year, with the finest exponents meeting to compare and evaluate new and previously little-known techniques and styles. I do not know if the event actually takes place, as being a foreigner I would not of course be allowed access to such a gathering, and by the very nature of the event there can be no written reports. Voltaire said that we invent words to conceal truths, so he may well have had the French Shruggers' Association in mind when he wrote his thoughtful essays about the eternal search for *vérité* and how best to find and demonstrate that precious virtue.

Slaloming my way through the maelstrom of gesticulating limbs and jerking heads, I catch up with Coco as he opens the door to admit the cold night air and expel his customers. As he takes my empty glass I ask him if there is a particular reason for his decision to shut the bar at this particular time. With the insouciant shrug he reserves for drunks, rude foreigners and tax inspectors, my friend explains that he has been invited to a New Year's Party at the home of a friend and that it would be very bad manners for him to turn up after the midnight hour has struck. He has already taken much more money than on a normal evening, the customers have homes and families to go to, and it will be nice for he and his wife to be guests rather than hosts for a change. While mildly aggrieved at this sudden change to our plans for seeing in the New Year, it is a sign of the time I have been living in Lower Normandy that I understand and even appreciate the logic of his actions. It is not the sort of situation one would expect to encounter at a typical British pub, but represents another of the reasons why we choose to live in this very special part of France.

As Coco and Chantal see us off the premises, I attempt to express my best wishes and thanks for a year of friendship with a carefully orchestrated shrug, but Coco merely looks at me bemusedly and asks if I have trapped my private parts in the carrot suit.

Obviously and despite my best efforts over the years, we still do not even speak the same body language.

Regrouped in the street outside the Flaming Curtains, my wife and I decide to make the best of our situation and demonstrate how Britons traditionally usher in the New Year. After explaining the basic rules, we link arms and lead the singing of *Auld Lang Syne.* Though the lyrics in their traditional form do not translate well into Norman *patois*, our friends join in enthusiastically and shutters soon begin to open along the High Street. They have not been opened by the owners so that they may complain, but rather to see what is going on and then to tell us how we should be singing the song they have never before encountered. Honest curiosity and frank criticism are two more Norman traits I love well.

Our circle is joined by more and more residents, and soon it seems the whole of St. Sauveur is joining in the celebrations. Miraculously, the church clock begins its unsteady chimes just as we reach the crescendo of the fifteenth chorus, and the participants need no instruction or invitation to exchange embraces. As he emerges from the crowd after apologising to and retrieving his new dentures from the wife of the town's principal baker, Jean-Claude comments that there are at least some English customs which are sensible and enjoyable. The mass kiss-in has also been good practice for his new career. He can now see the logic behind the final orgy of embracing as New Year's Eve is probably, from what he has heard, the only time that English men get around to kissing their wives or any other woman.

An hour has passed, and we are sitting on the ramparts of the town's castle. Milly the cross-collie is contentedly exploring the graveyard where our famous local writer rests, and from our elevated position I see that St. Sauveur is now virtually deserted. There is a lone figure standing somehow hopefully in the middle of the road outside the Flaming Curtains, and I realise it is Albert the Acrobat and that he is looking to start the New Year with a rewarding accident. In recent years he has avoided work and made a good living from becoming the alleged victim of any passing motorist unfamiliar with his routine, but tonight I think he will be out of luck. The last of the visitors have already been escorted to the town boundaries and seen safely on their way by an unusually friendly trio of policemen. At any other time, the traffic patrol would relish the opportunity to invite so many drivers to blow into their *soufflé*, but tonight have obviously decided to grant an amnesty. They are also probably aware that a French motorist with drink inside him and in a benign mood is far more likely to drive safely than when completely sober and in a raging hurry.

Looking out across the River Douve and the great flood plains beyond, my wife and I consider the promise of the coming year and review our situation. It has been another year of struggle, and we again came close to losing the Mill of the Flea as we continued our battle to make a living from my writing. Our bank account is as low, as they say in this area, as a toad's testicles and my plans for bringing in money with imaginative business ventures have all failed. But my wife has been as steadfast, uncomplaining and tirelessly supportive as ever and we have somehow managed to survive another year at the home we love.

The only shadow on our unexceptional but contented life at La Puce is money, or the way it seems to melt away when I come near. But, as my wife reminds me, we are still here despite my lack of universal literary recognition, and we are living a life which millions would envy. As she also reminds me, people with the trick of making and keeping money generally seem unhappy in direct ratio to their wealth.

I take my wife's hand and wonder again how I could have

been so lucky to find someone like her and how she manages to maintain her calm but boundless optimism and faith in me, my abilities as a writer, and our future. I whistle for Milly, and as we begin the long walk back to the Mill of the Flea I decide not to spoil the moment by reminding Donella of Coco's often quoted aphorism that while money may not bring happiness, happiness very rarely brings money.

Nationality has nothing to do with race.
Nationality is a thing like a church or a secret society;
it is a product of the human soul and will; it is a spiritual product.

GK Chesterton, 1906 - from an essay on race.

January

Dawn has long since dawned, but at this time of year sensible people in our area go to bed early and rise late, and I am presently occupied counting holes in the oak beam which spans the bedroom of the mill cottage.

On wet mornings, I count the frequency of raindrops as they fall from the ceiling into the chamber pot beside the bathtub. When the notorious Cotentin wind is exploring our corner of its domain, I count the number of times the broken shutter slaps against the bedroom window frame each minute. There is little to do on the land as we wait for Spring, and the rhythms of the seasons dictate our movements and moods. It is one of my favourite rituals at this time of year and day to think about all the jobs I will do when the weather breaks. This pleasant routine also wins me another few moments with my wife, cat and dog in bed. I have been promising myself for at least ten years that I will do something about the woodworm problem, but when I asked my carpenter friend Jean-Claude Goulot he said the best solution was to let my great-great-grandchildren's children worry about it. He reminded me that the giant and largely untrimmed tree trunks straddling the walls of our home had been doing their job quite well for three hundred years, and even Norman woodworms will not make much of an impression on them for another century or so. This is a common attitude in our area, and it is certainly true that many local houses seem to have managed to stay upright with the minimum of maintenance since around the time of the Revolution.

An impatient call from the hen-house reminds me of my responsibilities, and I look at the bathtub, consider my options, then dress quickly and go downstairs to set about my first task of every day between October and March. In our old life, the central heating woke with us and double-glazed windows and thick, fitted carpets insulated us from what lay outside our comfortable terraced house in England. Now and here, the old woodburning stove must be laid and lit and fed to take the edge off the cold and heat the water for a skimpy wash.

When we first came to live in the Cotentin countryside I thought the novelty and my romanticised middle-class urban notions of the joys of making a real fire would soon wear off, but the pleasure has stayed with me. I like my home comforts as much as anyone; I also understand that millions of people denied what are now everyday conveniences would think me mad to actually relish the daily chore of bringing warmth to our home. Perhaps it is a genetic echo from a time when a real fire represented survival, or just my small conceit, but I like the simple physicality of laying and lighting a fire; when I eventually grow resentful of the effort on a cold morning, I will know it is time to think about leaving La Puce.

*   *   *   *   *

The Mill of the Flea is now comfortably warm by rural Norman standards, and most of the smoke from the stove is finding its way through the tin drainage pipe which serves as our chimney. Donella is preparing our breakfast and Cato has gone off in search of hers. I wished our formerly feral cat luck as she swept out of the hole in the still-ruined end of the cottage, and more so for any creatures smaller and less ferocious than a beech martin which may have ventured on to our land during the night. I have already fed the chickens, fish, muskrats, crayfish, geese and other freeloading residents of La Puce, and am further working up an appetite by collecting wood in the copse by the road. Apart from this small patch of oak and beech, the wet and unworked land at La Puce is rich with elder, elm, hazel, hawthorn and dozens of other varieties of trees and shrubs.

The ten acres of fields and water meadows are divided into ancient and once individually owned plots marked out by thousands of yards of ancient hedgerow, and encompass a half mile of winding stream, three ponds, a picturesque cascade and water basin that we call the grotto, and endless patches of evil bramble and nettle that revels in feasting on human flesh and blood. Good fences do make good neighbours, especially in our part of Lower Normandy, and we are well insulated from the rest of the world. On one side, La Puce is bounded by a road where drivers test their brakes and nerves, while on the other, the tree-lined Hunter's Walk overlooks hundreds of acres of small fields mostly left to pasture or nature. We know those of our neighbours who farm their land for a living, but many of the smaller fields are owned by townspeople who do no more than visit them occasionally. The love of land lies deep within the Norman soul, and the ownership of a distant plot can be more of a status symbol than a new car. Ownership of woodland and the fuel it provides is even more of a status symbol, and I have to make regular patrols to frustrate raiding parties in search of easily harvested fallen branches, or sometimes whole trees. Unlike money, wood does grow on trees, but in this part of France the most desirable varieties for burning sometimes seem to have the notional value of a tulip in 17th-century Amsterdam.

Hearing the testy and familiar popping of a moped I disguise my pile of wood with a covering of dead leaves, mentally mark the spot for later collection, and hurry to intercept our postman. As well as saving him the discomfort of bumping down the heavily rutted track to the cottage, I will also avoid inviting him in for a breakfast of two cups of coffee, three glasses of home-made apple brandy and at least six cigarettes, which is the standard fee for learning the latest rumours circulating the area. There will also be news of Patrick the Post's latest collection of rare and cruel ailments, and a blow-by-blow account of how he has survived another night despite the demands of the sexually voracious Madame Megére. Normally I enjoy these early morning briefing sessions, but today I am anxious to get on with my work.

This time, I am not looking for excuses to avoid working on my latest book about our lives here. Rather than suffering from the writer's block that has plagued me in the past, the words have come tumbling almost unbidden from my mind as I sit at my table in the caravan by the big pond. We are as ever desperately in need of income, and a new book will hopefully generate interest in my past works. With the ever-increasing appetite in Britain for buying a home in France there is also the chance that a major publisher will at last decide to make a significant investment in bringing out and promoting my stories. Many thousands of readers have been kind enough to buy my books over the years; some even get in touch to say they cannot understand why I am so little known, as my stories about life in Lower Normandy are sometimes quite readable. What they do not realise is that nowadays, celebrity is all when it comes to bookselling. My wife thinks that I subconsciously want to remain virtually unknown as a writer as I fear that fame and fortune would spoil our simple lives. I almost wish that were true, but I also think it would be nice to have enough money to be careless of our bank manager's humour.

Our postman has buzzed away to complete his rounds, and we are at breakfast. Milly is hovering by the cooker and doing her impression of a Victorian maiden with consumption lying wanly on a sofa and direly in need of sustenance. Cato is sulking in the woodshed because my wife has refused her offering of a headless shrew. Fred and Barney the cockerels and their spouses are hovering by the porch door waiting for an after-breakfast snack of bacon rinds. Today, we humans are having fried black pudding with apple slices and cream to set us up for a busy day, but Donella always cooks a separate breakfast for our VIP guests in *l'Hôtel des Poules*, and their rinds will come attached to several slices of best back bacon.

Having left the official-looking envelopes (i.e. bills) for Donella's attention, I read her some carefully selected extracts from a week-old copy of a tabloid newspaper a friend has sent from England. Although we can hear all the latest news we need to know by radio, I particularly like the stories and features in the British press as they give a fuller picture of what is happening across the Channel, and of what the editors think their readers think they are interested in. A few moments with any British newspaper and we are reminded of what we are missing in modern Britain, and some additional reasons why we choose to live in Lower Normandy.

As the paper was published at the beginning of January, it contains lengthy astrological forecasts for the coming twelve months, and I see that my wife is due for what could be a traumatic year if she does not take resolute action. Warming to a general theme, the celebrity astrologer says Donella is being held back by an unrewarding and restricting relationship with someone who does not appreciate her. It will be much better for her future fulfilment if she ditches the encumbrance of this dead weight and at last realises her own true potential.

Noting that the four million people born in the same month as me are all going to move home, travel across water and experience bitter disappointment and financial problems in the coming months, I conclude that Mystic Morganna is having a bad air signs day and move on to the Healthy Living supplement. This section is also aimed at women readers, and is almost beyond satire as it even includes a cosily intimate article entitled Me and My Operation. The main item explains the importance of the ratio between height and weight, and even predicts readers life spans based on their size and shape. Idly jotting down my statistics and doing the necessary calculations I see that I have apparently been dead for at least five years, and ask my wife to add another slice of fried bread to the pan so I can recover from the shock.

I now turn to our satisfyingly thick pile of correspondence and learn of a man who is obviously an enthusiastic eccentric, which should go at least some way to qualifying him for a contented life in rural France. A retired policeman with a double-barrelled name that makes it seem as if his baptismal vicar had a stutter, John Harries-Harris writes to say that he is to set up in business in a village near Rostrenen, which is an old market town in the Côtes d'Armor area of Brittany. He bought his holiday cottage in the village of Bonen because it was next door to the bar and grocery store, and the widow running it had been thoughtless enough to die last year.

Accordingly, he has decided to buy the business, move over and set up shop as mine host in a region where even people from other parts of France can be regarded with suspicion. John tells me he has sold his vintage car to help fund the project, taken a part time job working at his local pub in England, and has even started doing the grocery shopping to get some hands-on experience in the trade. He is not fluent in French and even less so in Breton, but reckons that people are people wherever they are, so anticipates no trouble in adapting to a new life and business in a new country. He is also very fond of Kronenbourg beer and reckons this to be a prime qualification for the job.

Thinking the project through, he has even taken the thoughtful step of re-marrying his former wife so that she will be able to assist him in the venture. So far, he has already attended a two-day course in Britain on running a pub, but as the emphasis was on a smoke-free environment and other matters concerning good hygiene practice, he rightly assumes the information will not be of much use in a bar in rural France.

I shall write and congratulate him and wish him well in his venture, but will not mention the bureaucratic nightmare and financial and cultural challenges I know await him. Better he finds out for himself why all the small rural bars and shops are closing, what the Republic thinks of self-employed people, and why Napoleon so contemptuously referred to the English as a nation of shopkeepers. Having said that, I have long learned that my judgement on who will and who will not make a go at settling in France is more than suspect and that there are no rules of logic to apply to his or any particular situation.

My new correspondent also has a powerful closing argument to add to the strength of his proposal. Thirty years or more ago, he reminds me, all the corner shops in Britain were going out of business as supermarkets grew in size and number. Then, thousands of Asian immigrants arrived, took over the failing shops and made them prosper by hard work and giving local customers exactly what they wanted. Perhaps, concludes John, he is anticipating a similar phenomenon and one day virtually all the local bars and village stores in France will be run by British entrepreneurs. I look out of the window to see if there are any pigs doing aerobatics over the roof of the cottage, but decide I will not write and advise him against his venture. Instead, I shall suggest he keeps a diary of his adventures; any book recounting what surely lies ahead will be well worth the reading and may even be more profitable than pub-running in Brittany.

Next comes a jolly letter from a widow of a certain age who says she has developed an interesting and potentially valuable relationship with the owner of the hardware store near her holiday home in the Dordogne. Arriving at the end of last summer to find the loft had become an insect mortuary, she called at the shop and said in what she thought was reasonable French that she had a plague of flies in her attic and was probably in need of a good fumigator. After looking at her thoughtfully with his good eye (the other, she says she could not help but notice, was glass, ill-fitting and of a strange hue), the man had pointedly wet his lips, twirled his moustache in a decidedly lascivious manner and suggested that he call round personally to attend to her needs. It would be best for obvious reasons, he said, if her husband were not at home. Later that day, she told her English-speaking neighbour about the conversation and how helpful the man had been, and the lady explained why. The news of the English woman's visit to the shop had raced around the village after the shopkeeper had visited the local bar to tell his story. He had, he said, always believed that English men were by nature and temperament sexually repressed, with the women being consequently starved of their due marital rights. It was thus, he said, not a complete surprise to be propositioned by the attractive if mature new owner of the old Dupont place. She had arrived at the shop that afternoon, used what was obviously an English euphemism about having flies in her attic, then openly told him that she was in need of a good fornicator.

Surprisingly, my correspondent says that rather than causing a problem, her mistake in pronunciation had worked to her advantage. When the shopkeeper had called in his best overalls and clutching a bunch of flowers, she had told him that her husband was due to arrive from the ferry-port at any moment and suggested that he fix her leaking tap in the kitchen as an excuse for being in the house. He had made an excellent job and so far called on ten other occasions, and had been persuaded each time to do several useful jobs around the house as a cover for his visit. At the time of writing she had managed to avoid being alone on the premises when her would-be conspirator in fornication arrived, and if her luck and nerve held, she estimated that her holiday cottage would be completely restored within the year.

*   *   *   *   *

My creative session in the caravan is done for the day, the manuscript for the new book is nearly finished, and I am off to a meeting of the Jolly Boys Club of Néhou.

Donella is happy to see me go, as she appreciates that I need some time to relax in male company. She also knows that our regular gatherings are ideal sources of material for my new book. I know that she is keen to have me safely out of the way so she can begin her latest assault on the acres of bramble in the no-man's land beyond the big pond.

In recent years, the bramble has advanced relentlessly and my wife does not like being denied access to a square metre of her land. Being of the Norman variety, the ground cover at La Puce treats even the finest case-hardened cutting wheels with scorn, so as a special late Christmas present I have bought her an appliance that should be more than equal to the challenge. I had seen Donella looking wistfully at the new and very expensive scrub-burners in the local garden centre, and asked a fellow JBC member if he could find one for me at wholesale price. Didier Bouvier is a very general dealer who runs his business from a barn in Néhou which he likes to call his European headquarters. Didier claims royalty and foreign governments amongst his list of regular clients and although I do not know if this is true, anyone who can make a living from selling blank Rubik's cubes to canny Norman countrymen could teach the average British double-glazing salesman a thing or two about closing a deal. Although I have had my fingers burned in past dealings with him, he is a likeable rogue and if not always up to official specification, his goods are always much cheaper than list price. This, of course, is the key factor in selling people things they don't really need or want. Didier also likes to intimate that his wares have fallen off the back of a lorry passing conveniently through Cherbourg ferry-port, which is a further inducement to buy for any self-respecting Norman.

A week after I told him about our problem with the impenetrable bracken he said he knew of just the thing, and arrived at La Puce with a large, government-issue crate in the back of his van. Unlike the smaller commercial devices in the shop, the device he unveiled was khaki in colour and looked not unlike the sort of thing I have seen in newsreel footage of the D-Day landings. After admitting that it was, in fact, a government-surplus flame-thrower, Didier assured us it was unused and therefore as good as new. He closed the sale by pointing out that the prototype had been field-tested in the jungles of Vietnam, so should be more than equal to a confrontation with even the most overgrown areas of La Puce.

*　　　*　　　*　　　*　　　*

I have safely emerged from the mill track and on to the road which runs past the eastern boundary of La Puce. Once upon a time, what is now the D900 was used by little more than the grain carts servicing the Mill of the Flea, local people on their way from outlying hamlets to and from the village, and parties of pilgrims on their way to Spain to pay their respects to St. James. In those times, the holy route would have been marked by scallop shells and the history and significance of the old pilgrim trail are echoed in the name of our rival village, St.

Jacques de Néhou. For some reason, the French do not include James in their list of saints' names, so have settled for Jack. Nowadays the old route is light on pilgrims, and in the short time we have been custodians of La Puce the D900 has become a busy trunk route; to leave the tranquillity of our ancient and sheltered home and take to the high road is to become a time traveller and appreciate more fully how the internal combustion engine has changed all our lives.

After exchanging traditional hand signals with the driver of a Euro-lorry and waving to a bored-looking sheep in a trailer towed by a moped, I see a figure at the crossroads. He is waving awkwardly at the traffic with his free arm. With the other he nurses a radio which is so large it barely qualifies as portable.

I met Daniel Lebon and his radio soon after we arrived in the Cotentin. I was leaving the weekly market at Bricquebec, and as I turned on to the D900 I saw a boy standing at the side of the road. He was obviously engrossed with the old transistor radio he was nursing at his chest, but as he saw me he limped out from the verge. I swerved to miss him and, more in fear at what might have happened than in anger, I sounded my horn and shouted a curse. As I passed we looked at each other, and in that moment I saw that he was badly handicapped. The reproachful look in his liquid eyes stayed with me on the journey home, and when I realised he had been asking for a lift I went back, but he was not there. For the next week I drove up and down the road each day to see if I could make amends for my thoughtlessness, but it was to be a month before I saw him waiting by the roadside again. Daniel lives with his widowed mother in a hamlet ten miles from Bricquebec, and although we lack the sophisticated social services of more urban areas, our community knows how to look after its own. Wherever he is going, Daniel rarely has to wait long for transport. Now he is a regular passenger and it is good to share a cigarette and have him sitting by my side as I tell him about what is happening at La Puce and in our lives. He never speaks, but I like to think he understands what I say, even in my bad French.

I pull up and signal for him to get in, and find it somehow poignant to consider that, as the years have passed and he has become older, his radio has become ever younger and more sophisticated. My friend climbs in and I make the detour to Bricquebec. When we get there, we will play our little game where he has to guess in which hand I am hiding a ten euro note. He will win and be delighted, and as I wave goodbye and drive away I shall put the note from my other hand back in my pocket and know the pure and selfish pleasure that such a trifling act of giving can bring.

*　　　*　　　*　　　*　　　*

Turning off the main road and taking the winding route to our village, I toot my horn as I pass each of the outlying houses and am rewarded with the occasional wave from doorway, window or garden. Though it is January, it has not rained all morning and many villagers are taking this unusual opportunity to spend some time outdoors. Unlike those parts of rural Britain I have visited, people here still leave their front doors open in all seasons and seem to like fleeting contact with passers-by. Perhaps it is the natural desire of people living in isolated situations to feel somehow more in touch with what is happening in the rest of the world, or perhaps the owners just want to know who is going by. When we lived in a Hampshire city, I knew little more about our immediate neighbours than their names. But then, there were more people living in one long road than in the whole of Néhou. Parisians are not noted for their communication skills and warmth, so population density may have more to do with neighbourliness than culture.

Our club president and resident philosopher Jacques Délabré believes that national characteristics and attitudes can be traced back to just how close to each other any race traditionally lived. He says that the British and Japanese developed their formal codes of rigid manners out of necessity rather than instinct. Because of the frequency of earthquakes in Japan, people lived in wood and paper houses so it was important they had to at least pretend not to hear and see what their neighbours were up to. In such a small island as Britain, people began to live cheek-by-jowl and the same system of reserved social interaction developed. He also believes this is why the British are such an aggressive race, and compares our attitude when under threat to the behaviour of rats caught together in a trap. Before long, he says, they turn on each other to win food and space. I am not sure that this theory would bear much serious examination and I shall never be invited into most of the homes I pass, but knowing every resident in our village at least by sight certainly makes me feel more at ease.

Rounding the bend leading to the heart of the village, I see a figure on the roof of a cottage which is dilapidated even by rural Norman standards, and decide not to sound my horn. Madame Cochet is obviously doing some running repairs to the rusting corrugated-iron, and I do not wish to distract her and cause an accident. Although she has a fit husband and three hulking sons, Madame, like my wife, prefers to do all the maintenance work on her property and is acknowledged as one of the most skilful general builders in the area. She is also said to be the finest cake-maker in the region, and some of the villagers claim her experience with the ancient family cement-mixer helped hone her technique for creating the perfect consistency and texture of her *gâteaux.* Or perhaps it was the other way round. As she sees me and waves her hammer cheerily, I think about stopping to ask if she would be interested in giving us an estimate for the complete restoration of the ruined end of the Mill of the Flea, but decide against it. Until the new book comes out and our financial situation improves we could not afford even Madame Cochet's modest rates, and I do not know if Donella would approve of another woman taking over the heavy work at La Puce.

Parking outside the Bar Ghislaine, I sit for a moment to enjoy my surroundings and hear the completion of an earnest discussion on Radio Four. The programme is *Woman's Hour*, and the debate is about a recent survey. The researchers asked women of varying ages how satisfied they were with their lives and the results have obviously horrified the debating team, who are somewhat bizarrely described as 'dispassionate feminists'. In broad terms, the survey found that despite ever-increasing independence from their traditional home-making role, greatly enhanced career prospects and salaries, the younger women were much more dissatisfied with their lives than the older respondents. The panellists have different theories on why the young women are all so unhappy, but agree that, whatever other interpretations are made of the statistics, men must be to blame. Although I am no expert in these matters, it appears to me that this situation is a fine example of the Law of Unintended Consequences swinging into action. Although nearly all the women in our village lead what might seem an underprivileged and even repressed life when viewed from the other side of the Channel, it seems to me that while they may not be happier than most British women I meet, they are certainly no unhappier.

Before joining my friends, I stroll across the pavement to make use of the rudimentary *pissoir* alongside Madame Ghislaine's bar and grocery shop. As the bar has no other toilet facilities for male customers, it will save me a journey later and at a time when I might otherwise have to leave the gathering at some vital point in a debate, or more importantly, miss my share of a round of drinks. Now that I have persuaded our members that we should adopt the English tradition of taking turns in buying the drinks, some of our less generous members have adopted the ploy of ordering their rounds at opportune times. Normans are not known for their spendthrift ways, but some of our members are notoriously mean even by local standards. The legendary Michel Radin is no longer with us, and at his funeral one of our members remarked that we should have no fear that he would come back to haunt us. Even in his new incarnation as a ghost, he would certainly be too mean to give anyone a fright.

My time facing the old metal poster and guttering pipe will also allow me to window-shop for lunch. As I aim at the worn spot on the enamelled *Gitanes* placard while leaning sideways to look at an interesting display of pig's trotters in aspic, the door to the shop opens and two elderly ladies emerge. With my free hand, I lift my Mickey Mouse cap, and the two women nod in formal response. Small matters of courtesy are important in our community and I would not wish to cause offence by ignoring the niceties.

Drying my toe-caps on the backs of my trouser legs, I nod again at the ladies, ensure that my dress is adjusted properly, and enter the Bar Ghislaine.

*   *   *   *   *

After many years of painstaking research, I have come to the conclusion that the prototype for all rural bars in Lower Normandy was devised by a man in the grip of a terminal bout of clinical depression. In fact, I have a theory that the designer may well have been Edvard Munch, and if so, that he probably took the job to get in the right mood for his execution of *The Scream*. It is said that he gained his inspiration for that most desolate of paintings during a stroll in Nice on a January day in 1892, but I believe it far more likely he was in our area at the time.

Whoever was responsible for making the typical Norman rural bar what it is, the effect was to imbue the very walls with the distilled essence of his blackest moments, which would then seep out and infect not only the customers but the owner. In guide books and Sunday magazines in Britain, the typical French country bar is always depicted as an enchantingly twee rustic building with avuncular locals sitting on the sun-drenched terrace, commenting on a nearby game of *boules* as they contentedly sip at their glasses of wine. This may be a fair representation of the average bar in other parts of France, but decidedly not so in Lower Normandy. In our area and beyond, almost every bar seems to have been especially created to dissuade the customer from entering, or to speed him on his way as soon as possible if he does insist on calling in.

Regardless of the character and appeal of the building in which it is housed, the typical Norman rural bar will be as inviting as a dentist's waiting room and nowhere near as cheerily appointed. Floors will invariably be laid with mortuary tiles, and walls will be either covered with a style of paper that would embarrass any self-respecting Indian restaurateur; or painted in a colour that would make the inside of a refrigerator seem warm and inviting. Any historic beams will have been included in the standard ceiling colour of light chocolate or custard yellow. The furniture will come from the same design stable, and consist of wooden or metal chairs that make standing a comparative pleasure. I have even heard of inmates at our local Trappist monastery boycotting their nearest bar on the grounds of lack of comfort.

There are, of course, notable exceptions both in décor and atmosphere. The Flaming Curtains is totally unlike any other bar I know in the world with regard to interior design and furnishings. It also has Coco and Madame Chantal. My local in Néhou is far more in tune with the regional standard of appointments and décor, but it is my local, and also has Madame Ghislaine and the Jolly Boys Club.

Although the proprietor of the Bar Ghislaine is said to dislike men only marginally less than men drinking and, worse, men drinking together, there is something about her and her customer service philosophy that I find appealing. She can be sharp of tongue and acid in wit, but this somehow enhances rather than detracts from the atmosphere. There is no other bar within five miles of our village so the locals do not have much of a choice as to where they do their drinking, but I know that, despite their grumbles, they enjoy using the Bar Ghislaine. René Ribet says this is because exposure to the proprietor is like having a tooth pulled. The experience is painful, but you feel so much better when it is over. Other members of our club say that our host's treatment makes them feel at home, while the single members of our club say that she makes them appreciate how lucky they are not to be married.

For myself, I enjoy my daily encounters with Ghislaine. She may be small of stature and sharp of tongue on occasions, but has, as the local saying goes, more guts than a Breton abattoir. She also has, as we also say, a heart as big as the Norman sky. While a village bar and store is almost a curiosity in our area nowadays, Ghislaine has managed to keep her business going and is tireless in her efforts to keep the traditional village spirit alive. I once asked her why, as well as all her work in the bar and store, she dedicated so much time to organising all the community events. After a moment's thought, she shrugged and said she did not know, but someone had to do it although she often thought she must be mad. I replied that France and the rest of the world would be a better place if there were more mad people like her, and before bustling away she almost smiled.

Arriving in the bar, I see that Madame Ghislaine is already filling my beer mug and testing the bicycle bell attached to its handle. I also see that our club is in full session, that we have visitors, and that one of them is sitting in my seat. The male half of the couple is standing at the bar and I conclude that he is English, comes from the home counties, is middle-class and voted New Labour in the last General Election. Although I am a writer and trained by occupation as well as nature in observation, I make this deduction like Sherlock Holmes by first considering all the evidence then eliminating all other possibilities. The first clue in the evidential chain was the new and fashionable four-wheel-drive vehicle parked outside, and the British number plate and North London parking permit on its windscreen. I also noticed a faded sticker on the bumper assuring readers that things could only get better under New Labour. There was also a placard in the back window commanding drivers to keep a safe distance as there was a Small Person On Board. For some irrational reason I find these signs immensely irritating, and suspect they have the opposite effect to that intended. I have never seen a French version of the sign, probably because drivers here believe that anything short of actually nudging the back bumper of the car in front is safe and even careful driving.

Further evidence of the vehicle owner's class, character and voting predisposition is that he has a fashionably cropped skull, rimless glasses and a sulky expression which makes him look like a myopic and irritable baby. He has obviously worked very hard on his expensively casual appearance, and is equally clearly a fan of *serge de Nîmes*. His denim bomber jacket is worn over a pre-faded working shirt with no collar, and on his feet are a pair of designer suede workboots which have clearly never seen an hour's work. He wears no ornaments except a thin wedding band and an even thinner watch, and his denim trousers are so sharply creased I think it would be painful for him to sit down. Altogether, he looks like a man trying hard to look like he is enjoying the egalitarian company and surroundings, but would much rather be in a wine bar in Fulham telling his friends how wonderful it is to be in rural France.

The woman sitting in my seat is an attractive thirtysomething, but her carefully composed features do not completely mask occasional flashes of the irritated and exasperated expression commonly worn by the sort of woman who is usually married to a man like her husband. She is dressed in similarly expensive and *faux*-workaday clothing, and is doing her best to impress my fellow club members with her familiarity with their language and culture. As I pass the table, I realise she is talking about her admiration for the works of the great French writer and philosopher Albert Camus, and each time she mentions his name she stretches and emphasises the last syllable till she sounds like a cow in labour. This affectation was probably honed at any number of dinner parties in Hampstead but is clearly lost on my friends, who will not know how their language should be spoken in intellectual foreign circles.

I nod a general greeting to the table, then move to the bar to discover if my evaluation of our visitors is correct. My wife often accuses me of making snap judgements about people based solely upon their appearance and my prejudices, but I think this is unfair and argue that I just see more than most people in a shorter time and that I am generally proved right in my first impressions. To this, Donella invariably responds that I only choose to remember the rare occasions when my instant analysis has been right and that if people went solely by first impressions they would assume I was a self-satisfied, scruffy, chauvinistic and egocentric boor. This impression, I have to conclude, is obviously so far from the truth that it actually proves my point about the vast majority of people not having my eye for divining character.

At the bar, I introduce myself to the man and find out what it must be like to shake hands with a dead halibut. Our visitor tells me his name is John but without the 'h'. He is obviously concerned about this so I console him for the loss, and as I take out my tobacco tin he cringes away like a vampire catching sight of a freshly-sharpened stake. I take the hint and move along the bar, but offer my tin to Madame Ghislaine so we can catch him in the crossfire.

Before too long, I realise that Jon and his wife are prime examples of that division of the chattering classes which likes to think of itself as *bien pensant*. Invariably, I have found that people who claim to be right-thinking do not think too much at all. While his wife - who he says is to be known as Franny - moves on to eulogise what she calls honest and earthy rural French cuisine, Jon explains that they have stopped off in our part of Normandy to look for a new home after selling their cottage in the better part of Provence. In recent years, he says, they have been horrified to see what he calls the colonisation of their region of France by Britons. As he laments the loss of the traditional way of life caused by this invasion of unsuitable and insensitive foreigners, I reflect that it will be pointless to remind him that he and his wife are also colonists and that they are probably suffering from the NIMAC syndrome.

As with many country-dwellers in Britain who have got what they want and are now eager to pull up the drawbridge, the Not-In-My-Adopted-Country attitude seems to be flourishing in the circles of middle-class Britons who own property in France. They have found their favoured part of France and do not want to share it, especially with other Britons they do not think sophisticated enough to appreciate its pleasures. The affliction also appears to have a terminal effect on the sufferer's ability to recognise irony, as immediately after saying how the dramatic increase in property values in rural France is preventing young local people from buying a first home, our visitor cannot resist telling me how much he and his wife made on the sale of their cottage just outside Avignon. He adds that they are hoping to find a modest *manoir* in our area, which they hear has not yet been flooded with British buyers and will still retain communities of real French country people for them to mix with.

I assure him that nowhere in Normandy - and possibly nowhere else in all France - will he meet people who are more real than in and around our village, and particularly so amongst the membership of the Jolly Boys Club of Néhou.

*　　　*　　　*　　　*　　　*

Afternoon has become evening, it has begun to rain, and our visitors have departed. They are on their way back to the ferry and I do not think that they will be continuing their search for a second home in Lower Normandy. After Jon and I moved to the table, our club chairman insisted on introducing our visitors to Madame Ghislaine's best farm-brewed *calva*, and the couple were also introduced to the bill for all our drinks when they left. This is one local tradition at least that they did not seem to appreciate. They were also visibly unimpressed by an offer from René Ribet to sell them a time-share in the barn attached to his cottage, despite his assurances that the cattle would be moved out before each of their yearly visits.

Their final and most obvious disenchantment with the local culture and sensibilities came when Franny was recalling the perfection of a wonderfully simple dish of buttered Brussels sprouts they had encountered the previous evening. To a man, the members agreed that only animals and foreigners liked to eat vegetables. Indeed, said René, he personally looked upon Brussels sprouts in the same light as female pubic hairs. When confronted with either, it was best to push them aside and get on with the real meal.

*   *   *   *   *

Our visitors gone, the weekly meeting is now in full session. At the head of the table is our oldest member, Young Pierrot, and at his side is the giant JayPay, who is our secretary, youngest member and local celebrity chef. Beside me sit our president Jacques Délabré and my special friend René Ribet.

When we arrived at La Puce, René was one of our first visitors and he soon became my mentor in the ways of living in and off the Norman countryside. Through him I have learned much, and at little cost beyond money. In local circles, my friend is often treated with suspicion and known to the more respectable members of our community as the Fox of Cotentin; but as I have come to appreciate, who better to teach a newcomer about the lie of the land than a fox?

Asking after absent members, I learn that Patrick the Post and Michel le Scabeuse have sent their apologies. They are speaking at a symposium in Paris on the rare tropical diseases both claim to have contracted, despite never travelling further than Cherbourg in their lives. Our local general dealer and social events organiser Didier Bouvier is, according to a note he has sent, away on urgent business. His usual seat has been taken by a new member who is, even for our club, an unusual character.

Luc Voiron, like most of our older members, is of indeterminate and undeclared age. In our area, this means he could have witnessed anything from seventy to ninety summers. Also, like most of our members, he is not a slave to the concerns of fashion or image, and claims that too much attention to personal hygiene is an unhealthy and pointless preoccupation for a man of the countryside. Although this is not an unusual attitude amongst elderly men in our area, Luc is a special case, which explains why a seat nearest to the conveniently-open door of the bar is always reserved for his visits. According to club records, which are purely oral, Luc lives alone in a near-derelict cottage on the marshes outside Carentan that would be condemned under the Public Health Act if anyone knew it was occupied. He has never married, and says he is not prepared to go through the necessary refurbishment of his home, himself and his life to acquire a partner. In matters of relationships with the opposite sex, his shop, he often says when the subject arises, has been shut for many a year.

What makes Luc particularly unusual is his claim to be a direct descendant of Nostradamus and to have inherited the 16th-century seer's gift of second sight. Although he is highly respected in our area I have noted that virtually all of his most dramatic predictions have already taken place by the time he makes them. His claims to notable examples of second sight include the forecasting of the D-Day landings a year to the day after the invasion occurred, and naming the winner of the first *Prix de l'Arc de Triomphe* immediately the race was over. Strangely, his habit of making post-dated predictions has not diminished his status amongst our members and much weight is given to his pronouncements, especially when he is looking into the future to predict who is going to buy the next round of drinks.

As ever, the main and final item on today's agenda is progress with our continuing battle to win a significant grant from the relevant department of what used to be called the European Economic Community. Having learned of Italian farmers winning huge sums by inventing groves of olive trees, and Spanish farmers claiming subsidies for imaginary fields of rape, our club members are outraged by this foreign perfidy and naturally anxious to ensure that rural France should not be outclassed in such creative thinking.

So far, we have made representations for a grant to turn the largest silage clamp in the area into a tourist attraction along the lines of the Millennium Dome; for all members of the club to give up gardening and therefore qualify for setaside grants, and to make the local moustache-growing competition an official Olympic event and thus qualify for Euro-sponsorship. Today, we are discussing our latest application. At a recent meeting, I mentioned that farmers in Cornwall are now being paid to plant saplings rather than cereal crops in their fields, and there was an immediate motion that we should ask for parity with England on this issue. Although I pointed out that the Cotentin and its countless miles of *bocage* and vast forests is hardly in need of more trees, the funds committee persuaded me, as a local landowner, to draw up an initial letter of enquiry and send it off. Astonishingly, I have received a reply saying that my request is being considered and a response will be forthcoming. This ends our weekly meeting on a high note and I am officially invited to buy a final extra round of drinks to celebrate the good news.

*   *   *   *   *

Although it is raining quite heavily I have decided to walk the two miles home. After the noisy debating session, it will be pleasant to taste the night air with Milly at my heels and take the silent, overgrown and ancient paths which for centuries gave people living outside the village a direct route to the church and hopeful salvation. I will also have a good excuse to return to the Bar Ghislaine tomorrow to collect the car.

Before starting my journey I shall visit the churchyard opposite to call on our former members and tell them about the meeting and how our life at La Puce is progressing. I hope that I am not of a morbid nature, and anyway it is regarded as quite normal in our community to make regular social visits to the cemetery. On the day of All Saints, families will arrive to dress the graves of their departed loved ones with huge bouquets of chrysanthemums, and most will bring a picnic lunch. I like the feeling of continuity and acceptance of the inevitable rhythm of nature that this attitude towards death as part of life brings.

As I push open the old iron gate, enjoy its satisfying creak and pick my way between the neatly-kept plots I can think of few better places to spend eternity than in the centre of our adopted village, which, of course, is just across the road from my local pub.

Those who the gods wish to destroy, they first call promising.

Cyril Connolly.

February

I came upon a colourful harbinger of Spring this morning. A blanket of crocuses has appeared in the roadside copse. Individually, they are small, exquisitely formed, and appear somehow tentative like guests at a dinner party who fear they have arrived too early for good manners.

In our part of France, this is the time of year we call the rainy season. Some visitors to the Cotentin peninsula would claim that every season here is the rainy season, but this is unfair. With an average of twelve metres of rain every year, Mawsynram in north-east India is said to be the wettest place on earth and this is one record that not even the most patriotic Cotentinese would wish to claim. In truth, it rains here often because we are on a peninsula and the warm air of the Gulf Stream runs by the western coast. This is why the grass is so green and lush, and we like to think we produce the finest dairy products in all France, if not all the world. Another reason for our undeserved reputation as the rain capital of France is that the effects of a downpour are more noticeable in our rural region, particularly as Spring approaches. After the long winter hibernation, the farmers are re-acquainting themselves with their fields and leaving the evidence of their industry on track and road. The time of hard frosts is over and the land is softer and more pliant and has an eager thirst. The water table is approaching its highest levels, and the roadside gullies have become a network of fast-flowing streams. As they say locally, at this time of year every road has its own river.

Being an ancient water mill, La Puce was sensibly located in a low-lying area, downstream from a spring and at the confluence of dozens of rivulets that become coursing cascades as water is channelled down from the higher surrounding fields. Despite this winter deluge, we keep reasonably dry at La Puce as every square metre of the land surrounding the mill was artfully structured to direct water to the mill wheel and then away to someone else's property. Most of our problems with water come from it falling on us rather than boiling past us, but there are other minor inconveniences to living with a humid atmosphere and on a water course. It is impossible to use a salt shaker at any time of year, and the tidemark of rising damp is almost accepted as a decorative feature in all low-lying properties in our area. But at least we do not suffer from flooding, and unlike the owners of some nearby farms we do not have to go to bed with our boots on when the heavens open.

Though it can be cold and wet and we are still officially in the grip of winter, there are other more heartening signs that Spring is coming. Alongside the river, the towering beech trees lining Hunters Walk are still the skeletal hands of titans thrusting from the soil, but will soon be fleshed with blossom. The water meadow is no more than a sodden sponge, but the tips of ten thousand flag lilies are already sniffing the air.

While others go about their business of preparing their land for the season of growth, I am sitting at the grotto trying to calculate how many gallons of water are cascading into the basin as our river makes its eternal way to the Douve and on to the open sea. I am also trying to devise a way to harness the power of this thundering torrent. For centuries, past owners of the Mill of the Flea made a good living from the natural power of running water yet I still dread the arrival of electricity bills, and sitting here, it seems a bad joke that we have to actually pay for what comes out of our taps.

I give up trying to estimate how many bathtubs of water are passing through the grotto every minute, and start my daily trip to the top of the track to wait for the arrival of Patrick the Post. I have met him there so often during the past week that I think he thinks I am trying to avoid giving him breakfast, or that I fear he picked up a communicable disease during his visit to Paris for the tropical diseases symposium. Yesterday, he made a sarcastic and reproachful remark about lepers, and I noticed he was wearing a pair of cotton gloves when he handed me our mail.

The real reason I am so anxious to get my hands on our post before it reaches the cottage is more prosaic. What our postman brings in his sack could be of vital importance to our future and have a direct influence on whether we shall be able to spend the rest of our lives at La Puce. The new book finished, I sent copies of the manuscript to four leading publishers at the end of last month. As I of all people know, it is still too soon to expect a reply and an early response invariably brings bad news. But still I wait each morning for Patrick's arrival.

It is more than thirty years since I sent my first submission to a publisher, and I have become an authority on rejection in all its literary forms. Sometimes, a curt response will arrive within days, and sometimes it will be attached to the manuscript. For a writer with a script on offer, there is no more unwelcome arrival than a bulky package. Sometimes, a standard letter will confirm that the script has arrived and that someone will be looking at it in the near future. This will usually mean that someone will look at the cover before dropping it into the nearest waste bin. Sometimes, a personal letter will arrive promising that the sender will look at the manuscript in due course and let me know what he or she thinks. This response is both good and bad, as it will mean weeks or months of alternate bouts of unrealistic optimism and black pessimism until the bulky parcel appears; or does not. Occasionally over the years and as my books become more popular, I will receive offers from the smaller publishing companies. But nowadays, it is not enough for an author to just find a publisher. He and his book must be packaged and presented to the reading public like a new car. Huge amounts of money must be spent on persuading the media, booksellers and their customers that the product is worthy of their attention. Fashion is all, and the anecdotal memoirs of an ageing author living in France are clearly not in fashion. Or at least, not at the moment.

But this time, I believe it could be our time. For millions of Britons, the idea of living in France has never been more popular and books on the subject which have been promoted by major publishers have sold more copies in a week than all mine have sold in a decade. The modestly-published and promoted books about our small adventures in Lower Normandy sell well, but at a fraction of the rate if I were taken on and promoted by a top international publishing house.

This is why I have been waiting at the post box at the top of the track each morning. If the news from London is bad, I shall not tell Donella until I must; if it is good news, I want to watch my wife's face as I deliver it. She has been steadfast in her support of my struggle for significant literary success and the financial security which would accompany it. She is convinced that it is only a matter of time before we make the big breakthrough, and wants to be the first to phone our bank manager and tell him exactly what to do with our overdraft. Although I admire her eternal optimism, I sometimes think it would have been better if I had developed my career as a welder rather than try to make us a good living by putting words on paper.

                    *   *   *   *   *

Patrick has made a sullen departure, and I am equally unhappy
as the news from London is not good. One of the publishers
has returned my manuscript, and another has sent a card
saying that they do not publish fiction.

    Better news comes from my new friend and now
established bar owner in Brittany. The tone of John's letter is
exuberant, and he says that, while not making a profit in his
first week of trading he at least did not make a loss. I agree
with him that this is good going in the circumstances. John
realises that he is still in what the licensed profession calls his
honeymoon phase and that local drinkers will be calling in to
see what they make of the new proprietor, so is determined to
do everything to attract and keep potential custom. He
believes that the trick will be to maintain the traditions and
style of a Breton bar so as not to offend the locals, but also to
introduce the most successful elements of the traditional
corner local in England. To that end he is staging regular
music nights, alternating the appearance of Breton folk groups
with karaoke sessions. He is considering starting up a pub quiz,
but this will be difficult and even dangerous if a purely Breton-
speaking team were to be matched against a side speaking only
French. John has also placed an advertisement in the local
paper for bi-lingual barmaids, but will, he says, be looking out
for those with the sort of looks and generous figures that will
cross any language barriers.
    Finally, he reports that he is so confident of future success
that he has already started an extension to the bar. This will
require the conversion of an old barn at the back of the
building, and he has a cunning plan to harness very local
talent. The work will be done by the craftsmen who use his bar,
and John will bargain off work done against credit on drinks.
The workmen will doubtless inflate their bills, but as he will

only be paying half-price for the beer they drink on tick, it will hopefully be a win-win situation. He ends by saying that he is having all the work done in the evenings and weekends, so there will be no likelihood of official visits from the local planning authority. I finish reading his letter and reflect that, however his bar turns out, my friend is already demonstrating that he knows exactly how to go about adapting to local circumstances.

*   *   *   *   *

The rain continues, but I have decided to take my mind off literary concerns by working on the roof of the mill cottage. One advantage of the foul weather is that I will be able to see exactly where the water is coming through the original 18th-century clay tiles. Another is that we will not be disturbed by a visit from our nosy neighbour.

Mr Trefle has a farm on the road to St. Sauveur but seems to regard our land as an extension of his own, especially now that he rents a field alongside Hunters Walk. He told me that it is good additional grazing land for his handful of cattle, but I think he took it on simply to give him an official excuse to park his car on our track and see what is going on at La Puce. This naturally provides him with a fund of stories about the mad English couple that he can share with his drinking cronies in the bar at St. Jacques.

Like Mr Trefle, most of the local farmers think we are insane to keep animals for pleasure rather than profit, and are openly astonished at what they see as our profligate and wasteful ways. To be fair, it is understandable that some local people think us mad for choosing to live in the sort of dilapidated country property that most country dwellers spend their lives trying to escape, and especially for spending so much money in the process. They also think it bizarre that we should spend so much time and effort in growing vegetables, and even more so that we should choose to bake our own bread in a community which boasts three of the finest bread and cake shops in Northern France. That we actually spend money every week on feeding and attracting uneatable animals to La Puce is a constant source of bemusement to most of the local people. They also think us wanton in our other indulgences, and when we laced the roadside copse with fairy lights at Christmas, the parish council at St. Jacques organised a coach party to come and wonder at the latest example of our extravagance.

*　　　*　　　*　　　*　　　*

The deluge has eased to a mild downpour, and I am on the roof, conducting a fingertip search for entry points.

When we bought La Puce, one of our first concerns was to have a passably dry roof over our heads. Living in a mill, I reasoned, we would encounter more than enough water in our lives without wanting to entertain it indoors. After trying to find a local company which would re-roof the cottage for less than we had paid for the property itself, we considered doing the work ourselves. Then, one frosty January morning, an ancient moped came clattering down the track. The rider introduced himself as René Ribet, and said that he had been told we were in need of his expertise. He claimed that re-roofing old properties was his special *métier*, and that he could do the job much better and more quickly than any of the so-called professionals in the area. He would also charge a tenth of the best price we had been quoted. The conditions were that we would need to pay him in cash, not tell anyone he was doing the work for us, and the only materials we would need to supply would be two cases of beer a day for the duration of the job. As we were English, he would obviously bring his own lunch.

The deal was struck, I paid in advance, and when we returned from a week in England I was delighted to find our new friend on the cottage roof cementing a clay figurine of a wounded pigeon on what remained of the original chimney. A moment later, he came sliding down the ladder, declared the project completed and said that the pigeon was traditionally placed on a finished roof to ensure that there would always be food in the house. It was his personal gift to our future at La Puce.

When I mentioned that the new *couverture* seemed to be identical to the old one even down to the patches of moss and surface cracks on the tiles, he smiled and said he was sorry that I had not understood and appreciated the significance of what he had done, or the skill it had taken. Rather than destroy the character of the cottage by using new, mass-produced tiles or (even worse) imitation slates, he had actually (and at no extra charge) gone to the trouble of taking each 18th-century hand-crafted slab off, marking the underside with a number, then painstakingly replaced it on the brand new structure of joists, lathes and other woodwork. The beauty of it all, he said, was that the roof was now as good as new yet looked as if it had not been touched since the original tiler had done the job almost three hundred years before.

I agreed with him that, apart from the wounded pigeon, the roof certainly looked exactly as it had before. Climbing in to the tiny attic, I also pointed out that all the ancient woodwork looked the same, even to the undisturbed cobwebs and dust. With an expression teachers reserve for particularly slow pupils, the Fox of Cotentin explained that, as with the outside, he had wanted it to look as if the roof had not been touched so had replaced all the old slats and lathes over the top of the new ones. Such was the care he had taken in replacing the old wood, he had even managed to keep the dust in place. If I was not satisfied, he would give me back my money and write the job off. I apologised for offending him, and it was not till it rained inside as well as outside the cottage

46

next day that I had to admit to myself as well as to my wife I had been had.

When I cornered and confronted René in the Bar Ghislaine, he admitted that he had done little more than fix the wounded pigeon on the roof, said he had needed the money to pay a pressing debt and had therefore been a desperate man. I was English and therefore rich, and a newcomer to his country and region. Experience always came at a cost, and I had now at least learned never to trust a fox. We looked at each other for a moment as I considered my options, then suggested he bought me a beer while we came to an arrangement. One drink led to another, and at the end of a long session, an amicable agreement was reached. René would fix the roof properly when the good weather came, and make up for his trickery by becoming my consultant and agent in all future dealings with local craftsmen. As he pointed out, former poachers make the best gamekeepers.

That was twelve years ago. The roof still leaks, and the Fox is still waiting for the good weather. But in the way of country people, he often spends hours helping on the land for no reward other than a cold glass of beer and my friendship. He also nominated and seconded my admission to the Jolly Boys Club as the first overseas member and has taught me much about the way of life here, and about people everywhere. Despite our occasional differences, he is my oldest and firmest friend in the Cotentin. All things considered, I think I have mostly had the best of our many and sometimes irregular dealings.

*　　　*　　　*　　　*　　　*

The rain has stopped, so I lean against the crooked chimney stack, roll a cigarette and survey our little empire.

From my unaccustomed location, it is deeply satisfying to think that we own every tree, shrub, drop of static water,

47

hedge, field, blade of grass and patch of quagmire as far as the eye can see; and especially that nobody is officially entitled to come on to our land without our welcome. Under French law, unfortunately, we are only custodians of the river running through our land. In what some critics might see as a typical example of French jurisprudence, whereas anyone else is welcome to fish our river, I need a licence.

As the cottage is in a dell and our ten acres are ringed with either tall trees or hugely overgrown roadside hedges, the feeling of ownership and apartness from the rest of the world is enhanced. Some British visitors have said that they would not like to feel so cut off and would not want to be responsible for maintaining so much land. I reply that company and civilisation are only a short car journey away, and that we find the land mostly looks after itself if we allow it to. This is, I think, the best attitude to take if you are not to devote your life, like many British people who buy too much land with their French properties, to trying to keep several acres of land in the same kempt and pristine condition as their small gardens in Britain. I once received a letter from a man who came up with an ideal solution to this problem. Endlessly nagged by his wife to do something about the jungle surrounding their home in the Charente, he suggested they do their bit for conservation in the area by setting up a terrapin rescue centre in the grounds. A sensitive woman, she agreed, and my correspondent reported with great satisfaction that the family mower is now rusted solid.

Looking across the water meadow, I see a dense column of smoke rising from a field beyond our boundary of squat oak trees. Our nearest neighbour is obviously clearing the ground for the early planting. Perhaps he has also been persuaded to buy one of Didier Bouvier's bargain shrub-burners.

A harsh cry echoes across the meadow as two rooks settle a disagreement high above Hunters Walk, which is an avenue of lofty beech trees alongside the river Lude. Because of the rich pickings at La Puce, the waterside rookery is now as crowded as an inner city tenement block, and family and neighbourly disputes are frequent. Watching the squabbling pair is our resident grey heron, who sits on a branch of the Hobbit tree patiently waiting for the coast to be clear for his mid-morning visit to the big pond. When he first set up home on our land, I tried to dissuade him from using our waters as a convenience store, but over the years we have come to an understanding. I now turn a blind eye to his fishing trips as long as he rations himself to no more than a dozen goldfish a day. I don't suppose that he maintains his side of our agreement, but even a Norman heron would have a job to keep up with the birth rate in the fertile waters of the big pond.

Since the disappearance of our ferocious muskrat family and the exile of the male khaki campbell ducks, our tribe of psychotic goldfish has had few other predators and are once again threatening to take over as top dogs at the pond. The trout we originally dug the big pond to contain have long since been poached by the fishermen who think they have right of access to every drop of private water in their area, but even they will not catch and eat goldfish.

Apart from the heron and each other, the only other mortal danger threatening the fish comes from the descendants of Reggie and Ronnie the ferocious Cray twins and our feisty female duck Hen and her companion Ermintrude the goose. As with many members of our sometimes dysfunctional extended family, Ermintrude is not as other geese. Our balletic and good-natured goose is what the Chinese call a gift from the gods, and was waiting to greet us when we arrived at La Puce after a long absence. We do not know where she came from and did not make too many attempts to find out. After some fruitless attempts to find her a mate, she settled down to become a contented companion to Hen, and is obviously happy to think that she is a duck rather than a Loire goose.

As I survey the bucolic scene, my wife comes out of the caravan to give Hen and Ermintrude their mid-morning snack of maize niblets. The two friends squawk and honk in anticipation, slide off the islet in the middle of the pond and swim swiftly across to the bank. They clamber out and waddle up to the bench where my wife is sitting, then Hen flaps up and on to Donella's lap. Alerted by the noise, Fred the cockerel and his live-in lover Gert emerge from their hut alongside the grotto and take the path towards the pond. A moment later, Barney the bantam and his mate Big Daisy emerge from their luxury accommodation in the mill garden and set off in pursuit. Now Milly appears from inside the cottage and joins the race to get the best seats for a second breakfast, and I see the bulrushes by the middle pond shudder as Cato emerges from a covert hunting operation. From my position I have a pigeon's eye view as the cavalcade arrive and cluster round my wife. She seems to sense that someone is watching, and turns to look up at where I sit. I wave, and she responds. Even at this distance, I can see that her face is radiant with delight. Her husband is safely out of the way and at a distance, but within sight and getting up to no mischief and she is tending to her brood. Not every woman would envy the life she leads here at La Puce, but I think all would envy her her deep contentment at this moment.

The sound of a labouring engine distracts me from my pleasant reverie, and I turn to see a most interesting vehicle lumbering down the track. The ancient Renault delivery van has seen better days, but to a collector of classic French autos would still be worth more than the latest model. Contained within and lashed to a low railing on the roof is a teetering stack of wooden cages, and in them is a selection of hugely plump, glossily feathered and somehow haughty-looking chickens. From the sides of the van hang a miscellany of closed crates, buckets and feed bins, and as it clanks to a halt in the turning circle I see that a bicycle which must predate the van is strapped to the back. The last time I saw anything like this was when thumbing a lift from a bus in a rural province of India, but as the door creaks open and a sprightly figure emerges I realise that we are to be honoured with a visit from the legendary Chicken Georges.

*   *   *   *   *

I climb down from the roof to greet the founder and chairman of the Cotentin Chicken Fanciers Association, and reflect that what is said about people growing to look like their pets certainly has some substance in Georges Culin's case. I do not know what he looked like when he was a younger man, but now he strongly resembles and even moves like an elderly bantam cock. He is short and wiry, and as he approaches me he puffs his chest out, holds his shoulders back and sticks his head out in an almost pugnacious fashion. His rolling gait is jerky, and he lifts his feet unusually high as if he were hesitantly picking his way through a field of high grass or delicate crops. When he comes closer, I see that his sallow skin bears the pockmark reminders of youthful acne and that his prominent, beak-like nose is bright red, though I think this might be more to do with his well-known affection for home-brew *calva* than his lifelong association with chickens. The small and bright eyes are sharp and beady, and the overall similarity to an old but still sparky bantam is enhanced by the loose skin around his chin and neck which age and gravity have helped form into an almost perfect simulation of wattles. Nodding at me like a giant chicken pecking at the air, Georges takes his cap off and I am almost disappointed not to see a bright red comb on the top of his hairless head.

Although he is a familiar figure around the local market-places, this is the first time I have met Chicken Georges formally as he is known to prefer the company of chickens to

51

people. I know he lives on a smallholding at the end of a long track on the outskirts of St. Jacques, but I have never met anyone who has been invited into his home. His land is said to be surrounded by a high and impregnable wire fence made from the leftovers of German beach defences against the D-Day landings, and his cottage is said to resemble a giant chicken coop. Some village wags even claim that he has no bed and spends his nights dozing on a broomstick fixed to the cottage walls. Georges emerges from his giant chicken run only to buy feed, chair the weekly meetings of his club at the *salle des fêtes* in Bricquebec, attend shows and sell his eggs at market. He deals in neither live nor dead chickens because, it is said, he cannot bear the thought of anyone eating his friends or of sending them to a possibly bad home. He is a devout vegetarian, and as he has never been seen in a grocery shop or supermarket, it is thought he lives solely on what he feeds his pets. He has no family and has never been inside a church, but it is rumoured that there is a beautifully-kept chicken cemetery behind his cottage.

We shake hands as I make the usual pleasantries, and I notice his hands are bony, with claw-like fingers and long sharp fingernails. As I invite him into the cottage, there is an excited clucking and squawking and Fred, Barney, Gert and Daisy come fluttering through the gate to the water meadow and crowd around Georges like fans mobbing a pop star. He bends and gently strokes each of our birds, then issues a series of clucks and throaty squawks as he reaches into his pocket and produces a handful of grain. Whatever he says has an immediate effect, and our normally belligerent chickens stand quietly as he feeds and then examines them like a fussy judge at a dog show. Whether by coincidence or from instinct, he deals with each bird in the strict pecking order they have established during their time at La Puce. As he ruffles then smoothes their feathers, turns their heads from side to side and gauges their posture and stance, he grunts and nods approvingly, and I notice he pays particular and lingering attention to Big Daisy, our monster hen and undisputed ruler

52

of the roost in the luxury coops and sheds behind the mill cottage. Daisy was a gift from a retired English geneticist who lives in a nearby village and spends his days experimenting with the possibilities of dramatically improving the size and yield of farm animals by selective cross–breeding. For the past decade he has specialised in chickens, and the combination of his scientific background and hands-on experimentation has had some remarkable results. He also quite obviously believes that bigger is always better. Big Daisy is a dusky cross between several classic layers, is almost twice the size of an average hen, and sometimes lays three eggs a day. She also makes twice the mess of an average hen, and one can see why the manic breeder's wife and neighbours dread the day when he moves on to experiment with cows.

Having finished his examination, Chicken Georges explains that he has a proposition to make to us and accepts my invitation to come into the cottage for coffee and *calva*. Donella and Milly join us as we enter the porch, and I am astonished to see that our chickens follow us. Although I have never been keen on the idea of allowing farmyard animals into the house, I know that Donella has been secretly and unsuccessfully encouraging them for years. Now, they calmly strut into our living room, and gather round the chair in which Georges sits. I put the kettle on the woodburning stove and quietly drape a tea-cloth over the carcass of the broiling fowl we were intending to have for dinner. When one has visitors in our area, it is customary to ask them to share your meal, but although it is a very popular dish throughout France I do not think Chicken Georges will be interested in sharing our classic *poule au pot*.

*　　　*　　　*　　　*　　　*

Our chickens are back in their own homes, and Georges has returned to his. We dined on bread and cheese out of deference to our guest's presence, but the chicken stew will keep till tomorrow. It has been an interesting afternoon, and Donella is flattered to have received a visit from such a renowned fancier. She is even more flattered by the reason for his visit, which was to suggest that we might like to take part in one of the most popular and prestigious events in the region.

When we came to live in the Cotentin, I thought that I might become bored with the lack of social activities in the winter. I knew that the region was in apparently permanent *fête* during the summer months and that I would find it hard to keep up with the demanding roster of celebrations at every town, village and hamlet. What I had not realised was that virtually every date in the Cotentin calendar has some special significance, and thus is an excuse for a celebration of some aspect of country and coastal living. Apart from observing the dozens of gallic national holidays like Bastille and Armistice days, our region has its own long list of good reasons to take time off work. Throughout every year there are milk fairs, cheese conventions, flower shows, oyster and fish convocations and even a whole weekend spent celebrating the carrot and its contribution to the local economy and spiritual wellbeing of the area. Some uninformed people in other parts of France say that Normans are a dour and joyless race, interested only in saving money. They do not know just how active a social life we lead in the countryside of Lower Normandy, and I sometimes suspect that there is a regional conspiracy to finally arrive at the no-day working week.

As Georges reminded us, the major events of next month will include Cotentin Chicken Week. During those seven days, the region will enjoy marking the worth of the chicken and its place in our history, daily lives and especially on our tables. Few rural households do not have at least a pair of hens scratching around the yard, and many people in our area pay almost the same level of regard to the chicken as the Huron Indians accord the salmon. That ancient nation so appreciates the fish's contribution to their lives that they pay lavish honour to their main source of protein before cooking and eating it. In the Cotentin, we do not erect totem poles or hold services dedicated to the domesticated fowl, but Chicken Week is our more restrained way of showing due appreciation. The week is also, of course, another opportunity to put on a show and take some time off work. There will be chicken-themed functions in village halls across the region; schools will hold chicken painting and story competitions; parades will be led by men and women dressed as roosters and hens, and many shops will devote window space to a special fowl-flavoured display. Above all, the legend of the Cotentin Black will be told and retold wherever people gather.

Every region of any country likes to have its own claim to a superior and singular animal or dish. Yorkshire has its puddings, Bakewell its tarts, and Hampshire its hogs. In Northern France, Calvados has its eponymous apple brandy and its racehorses, Alsace its *choucroute* and guard dogs. In the Cotentin area of Lower Normandy, we have our weather, apples and their by-products, our history and our dairy produce. We like to think our cheeses are without compare, but so do the makers of the other three hundred and forty varieties found within the borders of the Republic. Other regions think that growing cider apples is not much of an achievement, and point out that our Norman history and unusual weather pattern is not of our doing. We were and are merely the recipients of both. This, I believe, is why so much is made of the giant and conveniently extinct superchicken with legendary laying powers. Although I have never seen or heard of any solid evidence, the Cotentin Black was allegedly once common in our area. Like the central characters in all legends, its feats and capacities and adventures have grown with the telling, and some stories actually claim that the Best in Breed at the Barfleur Chicken Show of 1066 actually sailed with William

55

the Conqueror to England and inspired him to win the Battle of Hastings. I have seen photographs of the Bayeux Tapestry which are said to show the great Cotentin Black accompanying William into battle, but to me it looks more like a badly embroidered charger with its hind legs hidden behind a provisions cart.

Regardless of the truth and origins of the legend, the Cotentin Black is the model to which all breeders aspire, and Georges Culin believes that Big Daisy is a natural candidate for the competition at Cherbourg. He had heard rumours about our giant hen from other breeders and fanciers in the area and so decided to visit us and see for himself if they were true. Although he is officially a resident of our rival village of St. Jacques de Néhou and will of course be entering his own birds in all classes, he is above petty concerns of rivalry when it comes to chickens. He will not be popular with the fanciers in his own village, especially as it is a St. Jacques bird who has held the title of Best in Show for the past four years; but having seen Daisy with his own eyes, it would, in his opinion, be no less than a crime for her to be left out.

After Georges left, we sat and discussed his offer. Though she is not in favour of any form of competition which might traumatise the losing entrants, Donella agrees with Georges that Daisy should be shown. Not only is the offer an honour to Daisy, it is a sign that we have become accepted in the community and that local people now recognise and accept that, despite our nationality and background, we know how to raise chickens. It will also show that her methods of treating animals like humans is not an eccentric folly. Although I see the logic of her argument, I am in two minds about the wisdom of showing Big Daisy. It would, of course, be nice for us as foreigners to take the top prize at such a prestigious and fiercely-fought event. It would also be guaranteed to ruffle a few feathers in St. Jacques. I suspect that the rumours about Daisy and her size and beauty reached our rival village from either Patrick the Post or René Ribet, who takes every opportunity to stir up animosity between our two communities. Whoever spread the rumours and as with all legends, the descriptions of Big Daisy and her laying prowess will have grown much in the telling.

On the one hand, if we enter Daisy in the show and she wins, Donella, the Jolly Boys Club and the whole of Néhou will be delighted. If we enter her and she does not win, I will feel I have let our community down, and our rivals on the other side of the crossroads will really have something to crow about.

*   *   *   *   *

We are going out on the town, and have much to celebrate. Tonight, we will be hosting a small *soirée* at the Flaming Curtains and tomorrow I shall be visiting the Jolly Boys Club to tell them our good news. After much deliberation, I have agreed that Daisy should be entered in the Chicken Show. Much more importantly, our money troubles could soon be over.

This morning, our postman finally delivered the news we have been waiting for, and we now have two major publishing houses interested in my work. The first letter came from the managing director of a company which specialises in publishing unusual travel books. He says that he had picked up the package containing my sample chapters from an editor's desk and taken them to look at while he was in the lavatory. He was, he adds, put in a spin by what he read, and compliments me on my unique style. It was, he thinks, inspirational of me to deliberately ignore the usual rules of punctuation and grammar and come up with a completely fresh and almost abstract approach to writing about a foreign culture. He is so impressed with what he has seen that he is considering departing from the company's normal style and presentation of travel books and setting up a division to publish what he calls off-beat work like mine. In closing, he asks me to send him the balance of the manuscript, which he will have copied and circulated to all his editors and fellow directors. If I will wait no more than a month, he believes he will be able to send me some good news.

The other letter with a London postmark came from a senior director of one of the largest book publishing companies in the world. He said that, of the more than four hundred unsolicited submissions his editors had been sent last month, mine was one of six that had reached his desk as having significant potential. Having read my sample, he found himself much taken with it as the stories brought back fond memories of his holidays in Lower Normandy. He would like to see the remaining chapters as soon as possible and suggests that I might call in to see him if I find myself in London in the next few weeks.

Having become, to my knowledge, the first local man to kiss his postman full on the lips, I raced down the track to tell Donella the news. I agreed with her that we must not count our chickens before even the eggs have been laid, but have insisted that we go out this evening to celebrate the fact that our ship has at last, if not come in, at least seem to be on course for harbour. While we danced around the sofa, I reflected that fate and coincidence can play strange games with an individual's future. It may well be that I am to become an internationally-known and best-selling author just because one man chose to take his holidays in a particular area of Northern France, and because another suffers from severe constipation.

*　　　*　　　*　　　*　　　*

We have arrived at the Flaming Curtains to celebrate the day's news. This afternoon I wrote to the managing director of the travel book company to say I would send him the rest of my manuscript and promise I would not finally accept any offers (however significant) from other publishers before he made his. To the MD of the other company, I said that we had already received considerable interest in my latest book from other leading publishers, but I would ask my secretary to put the balance of chapters in the post. I also said that I had to be in the Cotentin for Chicken Week, but would be visiting London shortly after the celebrations to appear and sign copies of my past works at the major French Property exhibition of the year. My secretary would call in the next few days and arrange a suitable appointment.

Donella is worried that I may be appearing too offhand with such important people, but I told her that one thing I do know about is how to negotiate with a potential customer. If I seem too anxious to do business with them, they may suspect that I am not really confident in my book; in the curious way of these things, that could devalue their judgement of its worth and how much they are prepared to invest in making it a big success. If, by my manner I can make them believe they must be the ones to publish my work, they will then have to spend enough money to ensure that their decision is seen to be the right one. In any business, the ultimate level of success of a product will depend as much on how well and extensively it is marketed, regardless of how good it is. This golden rule of business success as a self-fulfilling prophecy applies just as strongly in publishing. We and many of our readers agree that my books are at least as good as others in the same genre that have sold in their millions. As ours have not, the only reason can be that they have never been widely promoted. All I have to do now is persuade one of the publishers to spend a small fortune on bringing my work to a world-wide audience of readers and we will become rich and famous. It is not that I am particularly anxious to become a literary celebrity, but that will be the inevitable and necessary result of a publishing success. My wife will then have the security of knowing that we can spend the rest of our lives at La Puce without a single financial worry, and I will feel that my writing ability has finally been acknowledged.

*　　　*　　　*　　　*　　　*

Even for a weekday evening in February the bar is surprisingly quiet, and I see that none of our friends have arrived to help us celebrate our good news. This is especially disappointing, as I spent an hour this afternoon phoning round with invitations to join us. The prospect of a free drink would normally have even our French friends turning up on time, but tonight the Flaming Curtains is devoid of all but the die-hard regulars.

At the bar, I find Coco absent-mindedly picking his teeth with a screwdriver as he works on the clutch from his ancient Land Rover. Determined that we at least will mark the occasion, I order the best champagne in the house. I start to tell him about the letters from the London publishing houses, but he says he has already heard the news from Patrick the Post, then goes back to his tinkering. When I ask again about the champagne, he shrugs and says they ran out of stock last night while celebrating Albert the Acrobat's latest compensation claim. He does, though, have some bottles of *cidre bouché* that is at least as good as the fizzy and overrated wine from Champagne. It is also much less expensive and thus suitable for a poor author like me. He returns to his work, and hurt at his lack of enthusiasm, I remind him that a best-selling book which features his bar so strongly would bring visitors from all over the world flocking to his doors. Without looking up, he shrugs and sucks his teeth loudly in a very French way, then remarks that the town is already the birthplace of one of France's most famous authors, but it has never brought the pub named after one of his works much in the way of tourist trade.

As he picks up the clutch assembly and takes it to his

workbench in the kitchen, I suggest we go elsewhere but Donella points out that it is after eight o'clock so the other three bars in town will be closed. Then, just as I am about to leave in a sulk, a klaxon sounds from the kitchen and at least twenty people burst into the bar. They are all wearing masks, shouting wildly and banging on an assortment of pots and pans. One of them is holding a large and much-stained chamber pot, and at first I think that the news of my offer of free drinks has reached the bar at St. Jacques and the regulars have arrived to get their money's worth. But when the lead figure rips off his mask, I see it is René Ribet. As my other Norman and British friends unmask themselves and crowd round, René slaps me on the back and thrusts the chamber pot in my direction. I look inside and see that it is filled with cider, and that a peeled and brown-stained banana is lying on the bottom. The crowd begins to chant and I realise that they are recreating the traditional ceremony once visited on newly-weds in our area. According to local lore, the rites involved the villagers breaking into the couple's house on their wedding night, rushing into the bedroom and forcing the groom to drink the contents of a chamber pot that all the visitors had helped fill. To the certain relief of young couples throughout the area, the traditional ceremony is no longer practised. It is said to have fallen out of favour in our town many years ago, when the crowd broke into the wrong house and found the mayor in bed with the event organiser's wife.

*   *   *   *   *

I have emptied the chamber pot and eaten the banana, and we are crammed into a corner seat surrounded by an eclectic mix of locals and British settlers. Coco and René have competed to make the most moving speech of congratulations on our good news, while the Fox is now warming up for his Whirling

Dervish act, which he says he intends to perform while balancing the chamber pot on his head. As he has filled the pot with contributions from all the male members of our group, I assume he will be taking much more care than usual. By the fireplace, Madame Chantal is on duty at the cauldron, distributing portions of what she says is an English curry that has been made specially in my honour. We are being entertained this evening by a Norman-Irish fiddle band that has come all the way from Cherbourg. Their presentation of *Over the Hills and Far Away* in French with an attempted Irish accent makes for fascinating listening.

I start on my curried mussels and wave my spoon in encouragement at Jean-Claude, who I can see clearly in the crowd as he is wearing his professional suit of lights. The former carpenter and now apprentice *gigolo* is making conversation at the bar with a lady of advanced years and a very severe expression. She is at least six inches taller than him, but he is standing on the bottom rungs of a bar stool to make up the difference and they are at least seeing eye-to-eye from a physical viewpoint. Earlier, he told me that she is English, a widow who has come to the Cotentin to start a new life and is his first official customer. They made contact through the Lonely Hearts section of the *Manche Libre*, and he says that, despite her sour expression, he thinks she has fallen for him. She speaks reasonable French and already has described him as *joli-laid*. In France, this is a way of describing someone who, like the rumpled and outrageous 70's celebrity Serge Gainsbourg, is somehow physically attractive although definitely not in the conventional way. Although Jean-Claude is pleased with what he sees as a compliment, I think his companion may have been using the term in its literal English translation and meaning of 'pretty ugly'.

Elsewhere, our doleful folk singer André Déprimé is sitting on the corner of the stage and looking even more depressed than usual as Coco has hidden his guitar and banned him from casting a gloom on the evening. Donella is looking a little preoccupied as she is worried that we are tempting fate by celebrating our success at this early stage, but I am awash with the certainty that we are close to a final breakthrough.

Also with us at our table are two new friends with their own reasons to celebrate a big event in their lives. Tony and Louise bought a dilapidated cottage in St. Jacques last year, and contacted us soon after starting restoration work to ask if I would, together with their mayor, perform at a small ceremony to mark the installation of their septic tank and bathroom. Apart from a small problem when the contractor dug the hole for the tank in the garden next door, all went smoothly on the first stages of their project and the opening ceremony was a great success. Having invited the whole village to the *soirée*, Tony had brewed several dustbins of home-made beer and Louise had made a finger buffet, though there was some confusion when she tried to translate the term literally on the invitation cards. At midnight, the mayor had made a short address from the top of the new staircase, then he and I simultaneously cut the ribbon across the bathroom door and, standing shoulder-to-shoulder, christened the toilet basin to enthusiastic applause. Tony and Louise are clearly the sort of people who know how to adapt to their new surroundings and cultural attitudes, and are so happy with their new home and village that they are moving over to live here. As they tell me, the big decision came when Tony was unexpectedly made redundant from his work as a salesman for a shop-fitting company and what would normally be a minor tragedy for a young family became the spur to take the big step across the Channel. They have sold their home in England, booked their children into the local school, and will have enough money to tide them over till they find a way of making a living by working from home. Tony is a keen gardener and intends offering his services to other British home owners in the area. Louise is to continue her part-time job as an Avon lady, only this time calling on homes and housewives in the Cotentin instead of Essex. While there are now more British expatriates in our area offering house-sitting facilities than there are second-home owners, I think the couple will succeed in their aim to live here whatever they have to do. Often, I have observed, it is those with the character to burn their boats and take the plunge without a safety harness who make the most successful settlers. As Tony says, if all else fails, he can always try selling his body in the red-light district of Cherbourg. If he charges by the kilo, he adds thoughtfully, he should do much better than the average rent-boy.

Sitting next to the young couple is another new settler with a poignant story to tell. Gavin was a successful businessman in England whose world collapsed six months ago when he was diagnosed as having terminal cancer. A single man, he was determined to put his affairs in order, enjoy what time was left to him, and do what good he could for his friends and relatives. After giving his share of his business to his partner and selling his home in Kent, he put large sums of money in trust for his nephew and niece, gave his car to a neighbour and then moved over to live quietly at his holiday home in St. Sauveur until the end came. Two months ago, a specialist at Cherbourg hospital told him that in non-scientific terms, a near-miracle had occurred, and the cancerous cells invading his body had gone into retreat. Last week, he was told that he is apparently free of the malignancy, and, all being well, could expect a normal life span. Now Gavin does not know whether to be delighted that he has been reprieved, or desolate that he has given virtually all his worldly possessions away. He has received much encouragement in the community and the philosophic Coco often reminds him that it was probably the stress and strains of his old life that gave him the disease, and his new life in the tranquil hinterland of the Cotentin that cured it. As Coco also often reminds his customers, life is not a rehearsal and none of us knows what is on the next page. Sometimes it is better to follow your heart than make plans for a future which may not take place.

Now, another new member of our expatriate community is telling me a long and involved joke, and I shall need our host's assistance before I can appreciate the punchline. Andy is from Newcastle and has such a heavy accent that at times he appears to be speaking English backwards. To test my theory, I once actually recorded a conversation with him and when I played it in reverse it was only slightly less intelligible. Andy's guttural intonation and eccentric stressing on syllables also applies to his French, but strangely, Coco seems to understand him perfectly well. Consequently, I often find myself in the bizarre situation of having to ask Andy to translate what he wants to tell me into his version of French and pass it on to Coco, who will then let me know what our English friend is saying.

*   *   *   *   *

The party is over and we are back at La Puce, having a very late nightcap by the big pond. Before we left the Flaming Curtains, Coco took me to one side, gave me a bear-hug and said he was so pleased that at last it seemed I was going to get the recognition I deserve. As a fellow artist, he believed that struggle was good for the creative process, but there was no reward, as Van Gogh would agree, in becoming fashionable and acclaimed after one is dead. He is not able to read my books, but he knows from the occasional English visitor who has translated passages for him that I write with affection and heart about this part of France and all my friends here. Some of my stories may not be true to the letter, but they are always true-to-life. Anyone who has been to school can write, he added, but that does not mean they have anything to say.

Except for the odd grunt, snuffle or squeak from the creatures of the night, all is quiet as we sit in companionable silence. Above us, the vast Norman sky is cloudless and the full moon dances on the dark surface of the water as a sudden buffet of wind explores the water meadow. My wife shivers and I put an arm around her shoulder. It has been a long and sometimes rocky road from our early days together in England to where fate and circumstance have brought us. Apart from the obvious material rewards that success in my chosen career would bring, I honestly believe that all I have ever wanted is to make my wife and children proud of me. If all goes well on my trip to London next month, I shall at last feel I have fulfilled my main purpose in life.

Don't count your chickens before they are hatched.

Anon.

March

La Puce is emerging from its winter torpor, and we are preparing for what will be a busy and eventful month. Tomorrow sees the culmination of Chicken Week with the grand show and competition at Cherbourg, then I will be crossing the Channel to attend the French property exhibition in London and visit our new publisher.

Before then, there is much to do in preparation. Now that we are committed to entering Big Daisy in the show, Donella has been spending long hours at the hen-house. Apart from the daily grooming and feeding with a special high-protein diet, there are the deportment lessons so that Daisy will impress the judges with her poise and carriage. I know how important achieving a successful result is to my wife and almost everyone in our community, so have tried to help by teaching Daisy to obey some simple commands. For all my efforts, she seems to lack the temperament to sit or stand to my signals. I have even been on a crash language course with Georges Culin, with him attempting to teach me a number of significant clucks and squawks. But from Daisy's reactions, I speak Chicken even more badly than my Geordie friend at the

Flaming Curtains handles the Queen's English.

After her morning sessions with Daisy, Donella has also been trying to groom me for my encounter with the director of the publishing company in London. Comparing the relative effort and results, my wife says she finds preparing me to make a good impression much more difficult than working with Daisy, who at least has some sense of style and sophistication.

*   *   *   *   *

A sharp but pleasingly fresh morning, and I am taking the air and greeting our regular springtime visitors.

Unlike those who live in towns and work in offices, we have nature's calendar to note the passing months. Our land also likes to dress for the season, and this month the favoured colour is yellow. The ubiquitous primroses have been with us since December, and in the water meadow the rich golden flowers of lesser celandine are opening to greet the season and compete with the marsh-marigolds to put on a show. In the copse, nature is showing its perfect sense of colour co-ordination with a carpet of snowy wood anemones, their delicate and many petalled flowers shot through with veins of royal purple.

Although we have more varieties of flower than any garden centre and all come at no charge, Donella cannot resist giving nature a helping hand and the roadside verge is now awash with daffodils. Two seasons ago, she planted hundreds of bulbs in a special sequence and pattern to try and spell out a floral greeting to passing motorists, but the costly experiment was unsuccessful as they emerged as a profanity in the local *patois*. Despite the unfriendly message we had no complaints, and several motorists even stopped to photograph the novel display.

*   *   *   *   *

Mid-afternoon, and I have arrived at the Bar Ghislaine to report on progress with Daisy's special grooming and diet regime.

The atmosphere is unusually subdued, and I can see that my fellow members are deeply worried about how well our entrant will fare at the Chicken Show. Patrick Megére has zoomed over from St. Jacques and the bar which is the headquarters of that village's poor imitation of our club, and to his obvious delight he brings worrying news. Though he is naturally the sort of person who likes to deliver bad tidings, it is possible he is working undercover for our rivals. Although he is an honorary member of the Jolly Boys Club of Néhou because of his status as a postman and therefore the most informed purveyor of all scandal in the area, Patrick lives in St. Jacques and some of our members believe he is working as a double agent. They suspect that he has been passing information about Donella's progress with Big Daisy on to the St. Jacques Fancy, and he certainly seems to relish telling us just how formidable an opponent their bird will be.

According to him, the current Best in Show champion has never been in finer condition, and no expense has been spared on bringing her to peak condition for tomorrow. Patrick says the giant Rhode Island Red has been living in a secret location for the past month, and is receiving regular visits from all manner of expensive specialists. Apart from her secret diet, *La Grande Rouge* has been enjoying regular pedicures and massages, a mobile hairdresser has been giving her a shampoo and blow-dry each week, and a top personal trainer from Paris is said to have been advising on exercise routines to increase the girth and tone of her drumsticks. Our postman concludes his report by saying that the turf accountant at Octeville has opened a book on entrants, and the St. Jacques bird is the runaway odds-on favourite. Taking off his spectacles and polishing them somehow smugly, Patrick adds that Big Daisy is seen as such an outsider that the bookie is offering ten-to-one against our champion being even placed in the event and a staggering fifty-to-one against her winning the title outright.

His news is greeted with a deep silence, and I am so depressed that I refuse to stay for a drink. The meeting breaks up and I am followed out of the bar by Jacques Délabré and René Ribet. As he dons his cycle clips, I ask Jacques if he thinks it too late for us to scratch Daisy from the competition. Better, I say, for us to claim that she has pulled a hamstring or is for some other reason not up to competing in the event than for her to almost certainly lose against *La Grande Rouge* and our club and village be subject to ridicule from St. Jacques for months to come.

Our resident philosopher looks at me thoughtfully for a moment, then claps me on the shoulder and tells me not to worry. He is sure that all will turn out well whoever wins the competition, and reminds me of the truth of the Cartesian axiom that the only two certainties in life are death and taxes.

I shake hands with my friends and say it is a pity we cannot organise putting a fox amongst the chickens at the secret St. Jacques training camp. They laugh, and as I drive away I see Jacques take off his cycle clips, put his arm around René Ribet's shoulder, and escort him back into the Bar Ghislaine.

*   *   *   *   *

Disaster has struck, Donella is inconsolable, and it is all my fault.

When we arrived at the hen-house this morning to prepare Daisy for her big day, the door was swinging open, and she was gone. Her mate Barney was sulking in the hazel tree above their coop, and Cato was sitting on the bench by the grotto looking pleased with herself. There were no loose feathers or other clues at the scene, and no damage to the door or padlock we had fitted as a security precaution when we decided to enter Big Daisy in the competition. It was hanging open from the hasp, and as I saw the chickens to their beds last night the only conclusion is that I must have left it unlocked. Our other two birds were safely in their coop, so it looks as if Daisy must have pushed the door open and gone wandering off into the night. Or, perhaps, I suggest to Donella, we are *supposed* to think that Daisy pushed the door open and wandered off into the night. When we bought our hens and installed them in their luxury quarters last year, they immediately formed an escape committee and were extraordinary in their resourcefulness in spite of all my attempts to deter their regular breakouts. But, since they paired up with the two cockerels, our hens have shown no sign of wanting to wander from their luxury apartments and have got used to enjoying full room services and even breakfast in bed.

It seems to me that Big Daisy has been abducted, and I don't think we need to look too far beyond the crossroads at the end of our land to find the culprits.

*   *   *   *   *

We have arrived at Cherbourg, but without the Néhou challenger for the Best in Show cup. We have brought Gert and the two cocks in a cage on top of our car to take their minds off the tragedy, but still have no clues as to the likely whereabouts or fate of Big Daisy.

After spending a frantic hour searching every corner of La Puce, I raced to the Bar Ghislaine but none of my friends were there. Ghislaine said that they would all be getting ready to put in an appearance at the show, and added that I should at least make an effort to dress for the occasion. Even René Ribet was aware of the need to look smart for the big day, and she had seen him going into the unisex hairdressers at

St. Sauveur yesterday afternoon.

Driving out to his home on the marshlands, I told our president the bad news and suggested that we mount a raiding party on St. Jacques. He gave me a calming glass of *calva* and said this would be a pointless exercise. We did not know for certain that their chicken-fancying clique had taken Daisy, or that anyone had. Even if we did go to confront our rivals, we did not know where the secret training camp for *La Grande Rouge* is, or even if Daisy is being held there. He said he was sure that she would turn up eventually and suggested I go home and collect Donella and take her to the competition. It was too late now to scratch our entrant from the Best in Show event, but important that our club shows a united front and be seen to be seen at this important occasion.

*   *   *   *   *

The annual All Cotentin Chicken Show is held in a disused warehouse on the quayside, and like all such major events has attracted huge crowds. It is considered so important a part of our social calendar that the mayor will have attended earlier today to make an interminable speech about the superiority of the Cotentin fowl, and all the dignitaries from the *Chambre de Commerce* will be pressing the flesh, patting babies' heads and otherwise trying to secure their votes for the next election.

It is a fine and unseasonably warm day, with only a moderate sea breeze blowing from the harbour and there is an air of carnival about this normally deserted part of the docks. All regular markets in the area have been cancelled, and the traders have set up their stalls outside the main entrance. Many local businesses will close so their owners can attend, and few farmers in the area will do any work today. The town fire brigade band is adding to the festive air, and the temporary beer and cider stands are trading briskly. Unlike the many rural events I have attended in the Cotentin, there is even a line of portable toilets stretching along the quayside. A man with a megaphone is standing on a crate and keeping the crowd informed on what is happening inside, and the bookmaker from Octeville has set up beside the men's toilet block in what, considering the amount of beer, cider and wine that will be taken this day, must be a prime position.

Through the crowd, I recognise the unusually sleek head of René Ribet. He is talking animatedly with Mr Parier the bookie, or as he likes to style himself on his board, The Friend Of The Speculator. In case René has not heard about the disappearance of Daisy, I shout to warn him not to place a bet. Knowing Mr Parier, I suspect that if he knows Daisy will not be appearing he will still continue to take bets on her and then make some excuse for not giving the punters their stake back. René hears my call, turns and sees me waving, then thrusts a packet at the bookmaker and disappears into the crowd. I am about to set off in pursuit when the man with the megaphone announces that the *grande finale* of the day is about to take place, and we are swept along with the crowd as it surges through the main entrance and into the show ring.

Inside, the atmosphere is electric and I have to push my way through the crush to get us anywhere near the judging podium. As I should expect, nobody seems to object and I even get some admiring glances for my elbow technique. In my experience, when it comes to working their way through a crowd the French are beaten only by the southern Italians, and they are the undisputed champions of Europe.

Straining to see above the heads of the taller people in the crowd and those who are standing on chairs, I see that the stage is set and the white-coated judges are about to make their final selections for the individual awards for different breeds. I ask Donella if she would like me to find a chair for her, but she says she cannot bear to see the competition won by another bird and will just listen to the commentary.

While the master of ceremonies sets up and tests his microphone, the judges walk along the ranks of cages, stopping now and then to deliberate and occasionally ask the owner to take his bird out for a closer inspection. Then, clearly playing to the audience, the judges will make a great show of examining the bird minutely, and I see that each has a different technique as they prod and fondle and stroke. One of the older men makes a great performance of producing a tape and measuring the wattles of a fine-looking mottled hen, and not to be upstaged, another pries open the beak of his bird and shines a pencil torch inside as if he were at a horse show and inspecting the entrant's teeth.

Having walked the length of the cages, the three judges return to their table and go into a huddle with much elaborate arm-waving. After a satisfactory delay to build the suspense, each then takes a handful of rosettes and returns to the line of cages. Once again, every opportunity is taken to heighten the drama; rather than going straight to the winning owners they often walk past, then pantomime an agonising bout of deep thought before whirling round and slapping the rosette on the cage. Most of the owners are every bit as theatrical and some react like winners in a beauty pageant. It is quite bizarre to see sturdy countrymen clutching their breasts and putting their hands to mouths in mock surprise and exultation; one giant with a badly broken nose and livid scar down the side of his face breaks down in tears, then appears to faint and has to be helped off the stage by three officials.

The preliminary dramas over, the stage is now set for the Best in Show judging and awards. As our compere tells us while all the cages are cleared away, each of the winners of Best in Breed will now be paraded for the judges' inspection and marking. Then, last year's supreme champion, *La Grande Rouge* (who has of course not had to go through the elimination process) will take to the stage. Our host adds there will also be a special wild card entry, nominated by the Show's organiser and president, Mr Georges Culin.

Except for the occasional cry of a baby and shout of support for a favourite, the crowd grows respectfully silent as the lights are dimmed and mood-building music issues from the loudspeakers surrounding the stage. The compere clears his throat, takes a drink from the glass of cider on his table, lights another cigarette, then announces the first contender for the superchicken of the year award.

The judging process begins, and the first bird is carried on to the stage and into the spotlight by its trainer. The man lowers the chicken almost reverently on to the floor, attempts to get it to stand in a striking pose, then retires as the judges approach. While the compere is telling us the name, breed, vital statistics, family tree and favourite leisure pastimes of the entrant, the judging panel circle the bird, discuss its finer points, then make notes on their clipboards before returning to their table and handing their voting forms to the invigilator. He does a swift calculation, then takes a folded piece of paper to the compere, who opens it and reads out the score. This process continues until all this year's potential Best in Breeds have been assessed, judged and scored. The winner at this stage is a large and striking speckled hen entered by the Bricquebec Fancy, but everyone knows that the real star has yet to appear.

The house lights come on and are then dimmed again, and an expectant murmur runs through the crowd. Like the master of ceremonies at a world championship title boxing match, the compere now begins his build-up. As he reaches a crescendo of superlatives and shouts out the name of the reigning champion, the signature music for the St. Jacques superbird thunders out and *La Grande Rouge* is led on to the stage.

Though I am naturally prejudiced against her, I have to admit that it is easy to see why this bird has swept the board of prizes in every competition she has entered in recent years. She is a head taller than any of the other contestants, her coat shines in the spotlight like burnished copper, and her plumage is magnificent. An old hand at these occasions, *La Grande Rouge* obviously loves the limelight and struts around the stage with head held high before adopting a heroic pose and staring at the judges with glittering eyes and a haughty demeanour as if daring them not to acclaim her superiority. They make hardly a pretext of examining her, and after a quick scrutiny of the voting forms the compere announces that once again, the St. Jacques bird has scored a perfect ten.

It looks, says the compere, as if it is all over bar the shouting, but there is still the wild-card bird to be seen. Almost casually, he says that the mystery bird is known (rather grandly in his opinion) as *St. Georges le Noir,* has been entered by the Jolly Boys Club of Néhou, and replaces the bird that was withdrawn at the last minute. A wag in the crowd of St. Jacques supporters shouts out that, coming from Néhou, the missing bird was probably stolen and is already in the pot, at which the crowd responds with laughter and even hoots of derision. As the noise subsides, the compere asks that the bird be brought on, and then, as I strain to see our entry, all the lights go out.

For a moment, there is silence, then a nervous hubbub breaks out and the compere shouts for calm. As he calls for a technician to check the fuse box, a single spotlight high above the stage snaps on and a hush falls over the crowd. I stand on tiptoes, and through the bobbing heads get a glimpse of a large hen standing quietly in the circle of light. She is not as big or impressive as the current champion, but she is unlike any other chicken I have seen, as her glossy coat is coal black without a single blemish.

For a long moment, there is a stunned silence throughout the hall, then someone, somewhere in the crowd speaks two words. They are *Cotentin Noir.* There is a mutual gasp, then the crowd begins to chant the words and surges towards the sheep hurdles that ring the stage like fans at a pop concert. Just as it seems there is a danger to public safety, the spotlight snaps off and we are in total darkness again. When the lights come on again, the bird has disappeared.

Pandemonium breaks out, and a team of stewards have to be called in to restore order. Visibly shaken, the judges take only a moment to confer and come to their mutual verdict. As the crowd roars its approval, the title of Best in Show is unanimously awarded to the Néhou champion, the so aptly named (as the compere acknowledges) *St. Georges le Noir* and the first genuine Cotentin Black to be seen in living memory.

*   *   *   *   *

We have gathered at a bar outside the arena to celebrate our historic victory. The cup stands on the counter, and it is good to see the name of our village engraved on its base.

Most of the spectators have sped away to spread the dramatic story of how the legendary Cotentin Black appeared out of nowhere to steal the show, and the members of the St. Jacques Fancy and their supporters have slunk off to lick their wounds at their village bar. We know that their president put in an official protest immediately after the awards ceremony, but he was unanimously overruled by the organising committee. Regardless of any irregularities, it is clearly in their interest that the title and winner stand. There will be enormous publicity value and prestige for an event won by a breed that was presumed extinct, and secretly believed by most people to be a total invention.

Donella is obviously pleased that our village has won the title and glory, but also concerned that we return to La Puce and continue our search for Daisy. I say that I am sure she will have returned to her coop in our absence, but agree to leave the celebrations and drive straight home.

As we reach our car, I hear Gert clucking animatedly, then realise she is having a conversation. As we draw nearer, we are astonished to see that our missing chicken is in the travelling cage with our other birds. A quick inspection shows that Big

Daisy is well, and as her feathers are sleekly damp and shining it even looks as if she is freshly groomed.

We return to tell our friends the good news, and now that Daisy is safely back with us, we are free to stay and continue the celebrations.

*   *   *   *   *

It is late, and we are about to set out on the journey back to La Puce. Gert and Daisy have joined us on a moonlight stroll along the quayside and are obviously enjoying their night out. As a sharp wind has blown up, they will travel home in style inside the car with the champion's cup beside them on the seat.

It has been a special day for us all, and we have even had a pleasant windfall. Before leaving, René Ribet shook my hand and handed me a grubby envelope. He said that he had got spectacularly good odds from Mr Parier on the Néhou bird, and had put a few euros on for me. It would make up for the worry Donella must have suffered during Daisy's temporary absence, and the money would also go a long way towards paying for our leaky roof to be properly fixed. He would, he said, be willing to take on the job himself for the right price.

I shook his hand again to confirm the arrangement, and he smiled his crafty smile and winked at me before rejoining the crowd at the bar. Although I am a foreigner and from a town, I know he knows I am not completely naïve, and I was not at all surprised when I looked at my hand and found it smeared with the raven-black hair dye that my friend the Fox buys regularly at the hairdresser's salon in St. Sauveur.

*   *   *   *   *

There is a spring in my step as I walk to meet the man who may change our lives. In fact, I am limping slightly because I am wearing the purple platform-soled shoes that Didier Bouvier believes will enhance my presence at the meeting with my new publisher.

Although I am not known for being overly concerned with my appearance, much thought and preparation has gone into exactly how I should present myself for this vitally important encounter with a senior director of one of the biggest publishing companies in the world. Every afternoon after grooming Daisy for stardom at the Chicken Show, Donella would put me through my paces in the mill cottage, and we would role play with her taking the part of the publisher. While the chickens, Cato and Milly looked on, I would be made to knock on the door of my own house, wait for the summons and then go in for my mock interview. For more than an hour, my wife would ask me all sorts of awkward questions, then point out how badly I had answered them and tell me what I should have said to make the best impression.

Normally, Donella would not wish to be involved with how I present myself or my proposals in business meetings, but we both know how important this encounter could be to our future. Together with the coaching sessions, my wife gave some thought to what I should wear for the meeting. My proposal was to be as natural as possible, and so arrive wearing my everyday clothing. Our books are all about our life in the countryside of Lower Normandy, I argued, so what better than that I should be dressed as if I had come straight from La Puce after a day in the fields? This, said Donella, was out of the question as I would probably be refused entry into the building and risk being arrested by the police as a vagrant. In the end, we agreed that I should wear what she calls my writer's disguise, which is an old blazer and slacks together with a subtly checked shirt and fairly restrained bow tie Donella made from a half-eaten pair of curtains that a friend's goat took a fancy to when he brought her to tea.

I was also despatched to the unisex hairdressers in St. Sauveur before leaving for London, and have been instructed not to smoke, pick my nose, scratch myself or carelessly break wind while I am in the great man's presence. I agreed to abide by all her conditions, but have disobeyed her instructions as to footwear. She provided me with a highly-polished pair of black business shoes, but I am wearing the moon boots I was given at the send-off the Jolly Boys Club organised yesterday. When I told them at a previous meeting what I would be wearing, they all agreed that there was a possibility I would appear bland and therefore unimaginative. There should also be a hint of rebellion and even danger about me, and some small symbol of my contempt for convention. As Young Pierrot said, our famous local author Jules Barbey d'Aurevilly was renowned for his eccentric appearance and was a pioneer of the Dandyism movement in France. It was also fitting that I should be wearing some small reminder of our club and all my friends at home. Finishing his address to a round of polite applause, Pierrot presented me with the shoes. When I said the four-inch soles would probably give me nose bleed and that they looked a little dated, Didier said the added height would in fact give me more authority and presence. He also said that he knew from his trading contacts across Europe that the retro look was very fashionable in England at the moment, and most of the trendy young men I saw in London would probably be wearing very similar footwear.

Apart from the navigational problems, my feet are sore because I spent the morning walking around the French Property exhibition at Olympia. Each year, the event seems to become more popular, and going by the number of people flocking through the doors, there may one day be more British than French home-owners in France.

Another interesting aspect of the exhibition was the *salon culinaire*, where hundreds of visitors sat and watched breathlessly as a French chef sternly instructed them on the only possible way to cook a cabbage. Elsewhere, there were seminars on how to appreciate wine and even how to hold the glass properly, and the most curious sight was hordes of sophisticated Londoners queuing to buy French bread that must have been at least a day old. Perhaps they thought that all the specialist delicatessens and bakeries in their neighbourhood would be closed. As I watched, I thought about the prospect of staging a similar event in Paris, with eager French visitors looking longingly at photographs of ruined barns on the Yorkshire moors, watching demonstrations of how to make a perfect steak-and-kidney pudding and how to appraise and savour a pint of Boddington's Cream of Manchester Best Bitter. Perhaps I should think about contacting the British Tourist Authority to propose the idea, but I suspect they would probably think it was a hoax.

I have arrived at the publisher's offices, and am impressed to see that the company occupies a whole tower block. There is even a snooty-looking attendant at the ornate doors, so perhaps Donella was right in insisting that I wore my writer's disguise and not my everyday working clothes.

I check the card that bears the appointment time and the name of the director I am meeting, and after tweaking my bow tie and cleaning my shoes on the backs of my slacks, I straighten my shoulders, take a deep breath and try to walk in a straight line towards the doors.

*   *   *   *   *

A reassuringly familiar haze of rain and mist greets me as the ferry passes through the breakwater and into the harbour at Cherbourg. I have only been away from my adopted country for five days, but am feeling homesick. I miss my wife, my animals, my friends, and La Puce. Like going to the circus, it is nice to visit London, but I would not want to live there.

Seen from the sea, Cherbourg is not as attractive a port as some I have entered. There is usually a small flotilla of characterful fishing boats bobbing in the wake of the ferries as they shuttle another cargo of visitors to their starting point in France, but the ruined remnants of the German pillboxes on the breakwater are a sombre rather than inspiring reminder of recent history. So too are the dreary blocks of council housing that replaced what was left of the 16th-century buildings on the quayside after the D-Day allied shelling. But much of the old town remains intact, and for those who take the time to explore and get to know it Cherbourg is an interesting and welcoming town. A publicity brochure I saw last year spoke glowingly of the azure waters of the basin next to the fish-processing warehouse and the lines of palm trees which wave gently in the warm breeze of summer. A visitor, it concludes, could be forgiven for thinking he was in Polynesia rather than Lower Normandy. I think that the confusion would not be likely at most times of year and especially when the notorious Cotentin wind is whipping across the docks, but have never seen much wrong with a little poetic licence.

The ferry begins the lethargic process of backing into its moorings, and my heart lifts as I see Donella and Milly waiting on the quayside. My wife waves, and holds up Milly's paw in welcome, and I wave back and think how lucky I am to have someone like her to come home to.

*   *   *   *   *

An hour later, and I am still at the customs barrier. Because of recent events, the authorities have apparently decided to make at least a show of being concerned about who is travelling through the port. As usual, they seem far more worried about who they will let into France than who is leaving the country and for what reasons. Since the closing of the Sangatte refugee camp near Calais last year, other Channel ports have become popular gathering points for illegal immigrants and some cynical observers on the other side of the Channel claim the French are doing all they can to speed the alleged asylum seekers on their way to Britain.

I reach the front of the queue, find myself looking down upon the balding and perspiring head of a senior *douanier*, and realise why it has taken so long for a coach-load of French schoolchildren and their teachers to be allowed back into their own country. These kinds of delaying tactics would normally be reserved for foreigners, but apart from being French, the customs officer is wearing a uniform and a pompous expression. He is also very short, so demonstrates perfectly the origins of the English word 'petty'. As I am carrying a British passport and tower above him in my purple moon boots, I brace myself for anything from a grilling in the back room to an intimate body search. Thankfully, just as he takes my passport, tilts his head to look up at me and licks his lips in anticipation, a colleague calls from a nearby office, holds his arm up and points at his watch. Immediately, the flustered officer hands back my passport, waves me and everyone behind me through the barrier and scurries off. I look at a nearby clock and see that it is almost noon, which explains why this carefully guarded gateway to and from mainland Europe will be unmanned for the next two hours.

Walking towards the ferry-port terminal, I see a police car waiting outside with its engine revving, blue light flashing and passenger door open. The officers inside are idly watching the driver of a giant Euro-lorry, who is in earnest discussion with a group of swarthy-featured men clustered around the back of his vehicle. They are carrying an assortment of bags and rolled blankets and look decidedly nervous. As the customs officer sprints towards the police car, he looks at the group, then shouts sharply at the driver of the lorry. The man raises both hands in a symbol of surrender, then climbs into the cab and moves his vehicle closer to the edge of the quay. Satisfied their path to luncheon is no longer impeded, the dumpy *douanier* clambers into the car and it speeds off with siren blaring, leaving the lorry driver to continue his negotiations.

*　　　*　　　*　　　*　　　*

Donella is understandably anxious to know how my trip to England went, but I have insisted that I will only tell her after we have eaten.

We are in a bar opposite the ferry-port, and one which is a classic example of everything that is good about eating out in France. *Le Rendezvous des Routiers* is a small and generally unprepossessing establishment on the main road leading from the ferry-port and out of town, and certainly lives up to its name. The dozens of huge lorries which help turn the route into a bottleneck at this time every day probably deter many foreign motorists from calling in, but in fact the temporary roadblock is the bar's finest advertisement. Long-distance lorry drivers are the true gourmets of France, and apart from the finest quality and variety, they expect their midday meal to be served quickly, in very large portions, with a courtesy carafe of wine and all at a price which would not buy a pie and a pint in the average British pub. In the past twenty years of eating my way around France, I have had some terrible meals in the most expensive restaurants and some sublime experiences in the cheapest. When one breaks through the conventions of culinary pretension and snobbery, ordinary French people really do know how to eat well.

As we look round for a vacant place, I see why the customs officer and his friends were in such a hurry. They are squeezed into a corner booth, with their hats, coats and guns hanging carelessly from a stand near the open door, and every other table in the house is taken. All around us, large and contented men in overalls are attacking plates the size of serving dishes as they talk shop and compare notes on regional road conditions and the comparative savagery of traffic police in other parts of Europe. Frustrated by the sight of so many people enjoying so much good food that we will not be able to get our hands on, I suggest we move on, but we are intercepted by a pretty young waitress hefting a soup tureen almost the size of Madame Chantal's cauldron. When I say we are obviously too late, she smiles and shrugs at the same time, then takes pity on us. If we can put up with the mess, she says, we are welcome to eat in the owner's living room. The daily special is *finit*, but we are welcome to eat what the staff are having. When I ask whether Milly may join us, she says she has some leftover rabbit pieces which may be to her liking. Mentally notching up another two good reasons for living in France, I put on my most winning smile and tell her that I would listen to a Belgian comedian for an hour if it would gain me a seat at her table.

*　　　*　　　*　　　*　　　*

The meal has been a simple delight, and we are lingering over coffee. So far, I have resisted Donella's demands for a blow-by-blow account of my meeting, but the teasing has to end. I light a cigarette, call for another brandy, and tell her my tale:

When I was ushered in to the office of the publishing director and he rose to greet me, I realised that wearing my platform shoes to enhance my presence might have been a mistake as the head of the man I was trying to impress was on a level with my bow-tie. Assuming a half-crouch to minimise the difference, I stumbled over to his desk with my hand out and wearing what I hoped was a non-threatening smile. When we sat down I launched into my carefully rehearsed opening gambit of inviting him for lunch, but he cut me short and said that he would not have the time.

He then said that he had read the remaining chapters of my book and liked them as much as the sample I had originally sent. There were one or two areas that needed attention, but apart from that, he thought it was just about right for what it was. When I asked about how enthusiastically his company would be likely to approach the publication and launch, he said he would like to think they would be very enthusiastic indeed. If they went ahead, they would not, as he put it, mess around. It would be a major publishing occasion. Of course, he added quickly, neither of us should get too excited. Although he was the publishing director, with any proposal of this size and cost he would have to put his case to, and win over, his colleagues at the monthly board meeting. That would take place in three weeks' time, and he would let me know their decision as soon as they had made it. They would all receive copies of my manuscript in the next few days, and though he could not make any promises or commitments, he could see no reason that they would not agree with him that my book should be chosen as one of their flagship titles for the coming year. With that, he rose briskly from his seat and escorted me to the lift. As the doors closed between us, I made a weak joke about me perhaps becoming the new Bill Bryson, and he said he would prefer me to stay the old George East and advised me to get started on my next book.

Finishing my story, I squeeze my wife's hand and tell her that all we have to do now is wait, and hope that this time, nothing goes wrong. Apart from our champion at the publishing company changing his mind, running off with his secretary, getting the sack or having a fatal seizure, it really seems that, after all these years of struggle and waiting, our ship of good fortune is finally appearing over the horizon.

According to most guide books, Cherbourg has more than a hundred bars and restaurants, and I have done my best to visit each of them. All have their own individual appeal depending on your mood and pocket, but there is one establishment which is certainly unique. In Paris, Madame Zizi's would be located in Montmartre; our town's own bohemian quarter is to be found very suitably on the wrong side of the tracks.

Most tourists, British booze-cruisers and locals looking for entertainment head naturally for the centre of Cherbourg. Those in search of more off-beat surroundings cross the Turning Bridge to what was until recently a mostly neglected area of the town. Close to the docks and amidst a network of rusting freight railway lines and crumbling tenements, what was once a decidedly seedy area is now becoming trendy.

Young professional people and those with an eye to the future are moving in to and restoring the once-decrepit 19th-century housing, and squalid former council flats have become stylish apartments. What makes the area interesting is that the process of gentrification is not complete, and hopefully never will be. In what has been impishly dubbed the town's Right Bank, the old has not completely made way for the new. In dimly-lit bars once only frequented by dockers, merchant seamen and tarts, you will now also see style-conscious solicitors and estate agents taking coffee and croissants before setting off for work. While earnest discussions on the latest *film noir* are taking place over a cappuccino in a waterside bar, there may be a fist or even knife fight taking place in the alleyway outside. This sort of interesting social brew and its accompanying *frisson* of tension has always attracted artists, writers and other creative types. When I was much younger, my ambition was to live in a garret in Paris and write great works by day and spend my evenings at a classic *zinc* bar in deep philosophical conversation with fellow artists and thinkers. Nowadays, whenever I am in Cherbourg and in the mood, I head for the *Rive Droite* and Madame Zizi's.

*   *   *   *   *

As we are in town, we are to look up an old friend and fellow author who lives in a former bordello located opposite the police station. This, for reasons obvious to those who understand urban gallic culture, was a very convenient arrangement. Now, we are comfortably settled in a booth at Madame Zizi's, and Henry is telling us of his latest adventures. Despite his solid, middle-class name, my friend claims to be the son of a Polynesian chieftain, was educated at a public school in New Zealand, and worked for many years as a radio announcer and newsreader for the BBC. He was known for his deep yet mellifluous voice, authoritative delivery and immaculate pronunciation, and for listeners must have created an image much different from his actual appearance and character. He has, as they say in the business, a good face for radio, and is particularly, as his French friends would say, *joli-laid*. Like many artistic and thoughtful people, he is a natural rebel, and despite the Corporation's ability and inclination to absorb and convert non-conformists, he was eventually sacked for arriving late at the studio after a night out and reading the previous day's news bulletin to a bemused nation.

Since then, Henry has lived by using his talents to provide the honeyed voice-over for suitable commercial radio and television advertisements, and to present the occasional satellite programme on the history and culture of the Maori race. For these, he drops his given name and adopts the title of Kimihia Nga Rauemi which, he says, lends much more conviction to his broadcasts.

Henry is also an author, but tells us that, as a recent convert to Buddhism he is currently concentrating on not

88

writing a book about his life. As his interpretation of the basic tenet of his religion is to live for and in the moment and make no impositions on any other living creature, he feels that, by not adding to the boundless sea of literature worthy of reading, he is keeping his faith perfectly.

Also with us is a former BBC colleague of Henry's, whom we met recently when he appeared on our doorstep and said he wished to write an article about us. Wilfred De'Ath is the author of the most popular and unpopular regular feature in *The Oldie* magazine, in which he tells stories of his travels through France, overnight stays in the *foyers* which provide beds for penniless itinerants, and his encounters with interesting and usually much younger women. Wilfred is soon to have a collection of his magazine articles published, so we have further cause for celebration this evening. When we first met and after I had bought him a drink, he said that he had read one of my books and didn't think much of it, but at least did not find it as vulgar as so many works of the *genre*. He says he may review my next book, providing he considers it worth writing about. After getting to know him, I find Wilfred a complex and perversely endearing character and do not think he is as cynical, scurrilous and *louche* as he likes to appear in print. I believe he is really a sensitive man who has been hurt in the past and wishes the world was a better, gentler place. After a few drinks at our first meeting, he confided in me that he believes he has all the symptoms of genius, but not the disease. As Coco says, a cynic is usually no more than a disillusioned romantic.

There is a brief scuffle in the corner of the bar, and we watch as a small, rat-like man is helped through the doorway by the proprietor. Having seen him on his way, Madame Zizi joins us and explains that her victim is a notorious local *frotteur*. This common street expression comes from the verb 'to rub', and describes perfectly the sort of man who likes to press himself against women while in crowded locations. Adjusting her shoulder strap, our hostess explains that this would not normally cause much of a stir in her bar, but the man was so drunk he could not see straight and had mistakenly practised his hobby on a burly docker rather than the girl standing beside him.

Going by her stories of life in the red-light district during the last war, our hostess must be of very advanced years, but it is hard to tell Madame Zizi's age as her extravagantly bouffanted wig is sleekly black and her face plastered with a thick layer of bone-white make-up. With her deadpan features, expressive gestures and dressed in one of the ornate and flowing evening dresses she habitually wears, she looks to me exactly like a performer in a Japanese *kabuki* play.

We spend a few moments talking about life and where we think we are all going as we journey through it, then Madame Zizi hears of our good news and decides it is time that I have my first experience of *absinthe*. She is surprised that someone like me has never tried the traditional drink of French writers, and believes familiarity with its effects may inspire me to even better work.

I make a show of resistance, but as the long glass, tall spoon, sugar cubes and secret bottle is brought to our table, I concede. It is obviously going to be a night to remember. Or perhaps not.

*   *   *   *   *

Early the next day, and I am feeling a little delicate. But in spite of the aftermath of my initiation to the drink of choice of some of the greatest and maddest French writers, I am in a buoyant mood. When it was clear that we were in for a long session at Madame Zizi's, Donella called a friendly neighbour and asked her to see the chickens safely to bed, and we spent the night on the floor of Henry's apartment. We could have found a hotel, but my wife did not think I was fit for exposure to civilised society. She also said it would save money, and anyway, the sleeping arrangements made a suitable finale to our bohemian evening.

Although I much prefer living in the countryside, I like to feel pavements under my feet at regular intervals and particularly enjoy walking the streets as Cherbourg wakes.

As we make our way across the Turning Bridge to where we left our car the previous evening, gulls wheel overhead and seem to be laughing harshly at some private joke as they swoop down to seek pickings in the overflowing bins outside restaurants and bars. The occasional car races by in search of an unwary cyclist or pedestrian, and small groups of dishevelled Britons look for an English-style pub that is open so they can refuel before catching the early morning ferry back to their real worlds. Although it has not been raining, the pavements gleam from the attentions of a council worker astride his ingenious water-spraying machine, and trolleys of fresh fruit, vegetables and fish are being wheeled into shops along the quayside. I breathe in the morning air, and savour the heady fusion of aromas coming from the sea, freshly-brewed coffee, baking bread, stale tobacco and urine which means we could be nowhere else in the world but a French port.

Arriving in the *Place du Théâtre*, I am reminded that it is market day, and see that our car has metamorphosed overnight into a sausage stall. I ask the owner if he has seen a white English car in the vicinity, and he says he has seen no white cars of any nationality this morning. I remember Donella's current experiments with growing a moss culture on Victor's bodywork, and ask him if he has seen a green car with English number plates.

The man concentrates on tying a bunch of bright red *saucissons* on a pole above his head, then says that, now he thinks of it, he does remember the foreign wreck that was occupying the place he and his family have been trading from every market day for the past century. I take the hint and buy a brace of large and odiferous salamis, and he tells me that the police responded to his call an hour ago and came and towed it away. I could try the *gendarmerie*, but bearing in mind the condition of our car, he suggests we might try the town scrap heap first.

Realising what the gulls were laughing about, we start on one of the salamis as we retrace our route across the bridge. At the police station, a fat policeman eating a croissant directs us to the traffic department, where an even fatter policeman is eating a filled baguette the size of the riot baton on his desk. We tell him our problem and he suggests we try the compound behind the station.

There, we find a group of officers clustered around poor Victor, who is hanging forlornly from a tow-truck. One of them is testing the play of the front wheels with his boot and another is poking a penknife through the thinner part of the bodywork. Another whistles in amazement and almost awe as he inspects the remains of the exhaust system, and I begin to tally up the likely total of fines which could be impending, quite apart from the cost of the parking violation.

Offering the sergeant a bite of my salami I decide to come clean, and explain that we live in the countryside near St. Sauveur and I, as an author who writes solely about the Cotentin and how it is the finest area in all France, had spent the previous evening seeking inspiration at Madame Zizi's where I was introduced to and fell foul of a litre bottle of *absinthe*.

This is not the line one would take with a traffic officer in Britain, but we are in France. After writing down his name so I would spell it properly in my next book, Sergeant Guy Lecroix shakes my hand, wishes us a safe voyage home and orders that Victor be lowered from the back of the tow-truck and our parking ticket torn up.

I thank him for his courtesy and indulgence, and as we

climb into Victor and start our journey back to the tranquillity of La Puce I think how good it is to live in a country where the pursuit and exercise of personal liberty and creativity is often seen as much more important than observing the letter of the law.

Wise men learn by other men's mistakes; fools, by their own.

Anon.

April

Another week must drag by before we can expect to hear from London. The travel book company has been in touch to make us a modest offer, but despite Donella's reservations I have replied that we are expecting a much better and bigger proposal.

At La Puce, the days grow longer as nature's yearly cycle rolls by. A single-parent wren has set up home in a hole in a wall at the ruined end of the mill cottage, and as this will be the fourth year that she has chosen to trust us and bring up her family under our protection, we feel the responsibility. All wrens look much alike to me, but Donella has inspected the construction of the perfectly-formed nest and says she recognises the weave and style, so it must be the same bird.

Normally at this time of year, we would be trying to enforce a Cato exclusion zone around all the nesting areas at La Puce, but our werecat appears disinterested in the prospects of torture and murder on a grand scale. In recent weeks, she seems to have grown ever more lethargic and now spends most of her time lying in the woodshed on an old pair of trousers that even I consider beyond use. Our once ferocious cat has lost weight, and her luxuriant coat is becoming increasingly drab and patchy. Although Donella says it is only her winter fur moulting, I know she is concerned about the feral cat that came out of a storm and in to our lives four years ago.

Together with Cato's indisposition, my wife is also worried about the balance of relationships at the chicken run. Now that Big Daisy is the current all-Cotentin superchicken, her head has been turned as a result of all the publicity and attention she is receiving. Apart from a photograph and story about her appearing on the front page of the local newspaper and her interview with a reporter from Cherbourg Radio, she is now receiving fan mail from chicken fanciers across the region - and even proposals of marriage. These are allegedly written by lovelorn cockerels, but have obviously been fabricated by owners who want to breed from our famous chicken. We are also receiving regular calls and letters from associations who want to book Daisy to make a personal appearance at their summer shows. Now, there is even talk of setting up a fan club with its own website so that enthusiasts from around the world can learn of her daily routine, favourite food, colour schemes and pop music. The most curious aspect of the whole affair is that nobody seems concerned that our hen is no longer posing as a true Cotentin Black.

When I told René Ribet about the furore and said we would be stripped of the title and have to return the cup when his trickery with the hair dye was exposed, he smiled and said that people only see what they want to see. It suited everyone to believe that Daisy was a Cotentin Black, and human nature would ensure that nobody would point out that she is actually an attractive but quite ordinary mottled hen. If singers who cannot sing, artists who cannot paint and politicians who don't care about people can become rich and famous, why not a hen who is not really what we claim her to be? If I was worried about it, he said, he could arrange for a weekly colouring session to take place in the hen-house, then we could open La Puce to the public and charge people to see the famous bird. Although this seemed a good money-making scheme to me, Donella says she is having quite enough trouble with our celebrity chicken as it is. Now that our hen is acting like a film star, the old problems with infidelity have resurfaced, and we suspect the torrid affair between Big Daisy and Gert's partner Fred has re-ignited. If Barney finds out what is going on, there is bound to be trouble between the two cocks, and Daisy is now so famous that the salacious details would probably be splashed across the pages of the more scurrilous of our regional journals.

*   *   *   *   *

Another big date in the Cotentin calendar has arrived, and we are off to the Tree Fair at Sourciéville. As anyone who has driven through the *bocage* region will know, Normans are fond of trees. Trees as forests mean cover for game, and one of William the Conqueror's first jobs when setting up shop in England was to plant the vast New Forest in Hampshire. Trees as firewood also spell warmth and comfort during the long Norman winter, and so trees as possessions mean added status. This is why the market square at Sourciéville will be forested with saplings of every size and variety over the weekend, and many hundreds of Cotentinese will overcome their prejudices to visit the town.

Although it is a perfectly normal-looking place and the people who live there seem much the same as elsewhere, Sourciéville is said to have a dark history. The town is at the centre of the great swathe of marshlands which bisect the peninsula, and for most of the winter it is ringed and virtually isolated by what the Cotentinese call the inland sea. The same families have lived there for centuries, and outsiders, except during Tree Fair week when there is good money to be had from them, are not welcome.

Consequently, Sourciéville has acquired a reputation as

being a hotbed of strange and often supernatural practices and events. There are rumours of sinister rituals and rites by full moonlight, and unholy gatherings on the marshes at certain times of the year. Goats and cats are allegedly the pets of choice in the town, the local hardware store specialises in hand-made besom brooms, and it is said that chickens and virgins are always in short supply. While I have never seen or heard of any practical evidence of witchcraft or necromancy practised by its community, I can see how and why the town has become the focus for such allegations. An academic friend of mine has written and published a paper on the Cotentin, and in it he argues that all great tracts of flat and featureless marshy terrain naturally attract myths and tales of the supernatural. With its location, appearance and general ambience, Sourciéville fits within his parameters perfectly. The only abandoned church I know of in the whole region lies just outside the town, and the area seems permanently swathed in a miasma of particularly dramatic and clammy mist. Surrounded as it is by water this is hardly surprising in winter, but there is a regional saying that the sun never shines in Sourciéville, whatever the weather elsewhere.

*   *   *   *   *

We have arrived at the Tree Fair, but not without incident. I had forgotten that the regional baton-dropping championships are also taking place this weekend, and all cars are being diverted around Gaucheville. The annual festival of Joan of Arc is to be staged at Bigosville on Monday, and this has given the re-enactment committee a good excuse to block off the through-road while they are busy erecting the stake and faggots in the square. There is a short diversion for French drivers, but with the natural anti-English fervour this event encourages, cars with British number plates are often directed on a special route which is guaranteed to take their owners miles out of their way. But we have become used to these regular exercises in unilateral traffic management, and know it is part of the fun of any special occasion. From now until the end of summer, towns and villages all over the region will be summarily setting up roadblocks and even charging travellers a levy to pass through the boundaries if a *fête* or special event is going on. In my experience, the French have little respect for the sanctity of the public highway, and this cavalier attitude is demonstrated most clearly when the next excuse for a national haulage operators' strike arrives.

As we look for a parking place, I am especially wary when we approach any major or minor road junctions, or any passage from which a car could conceivably emerge. Most isolated towns in our region have developed their own attitude to and application of the national rules of the road, but Sourciéville is in a class of its own. Virtually all the locals observe the now extinct requirement of giving way to vehicles emerging from the right, but most choose not to conform if encountering a car driven by an enemy, visitor or foreigner. With such a major event taking place in the town, confusion naturally reigns and driving in Sourciéville today would bring the most battle-hardened Parisian taxi driver out in a sweat.

Following two near-misses and an invigorating bumper-to-bumper confrontation with an elderly lady with a squint who literally cursed me as I backed away, I manage to find a space, and we set off for the square. Although I like trees, we have several hundred at La Puce so I do not understand my wife's enthusiasm for buying and planting even more. Donella knows my views and suggests that I go off and amuse myself for a couple of hours, which is our code for my finding a bar and getting to know the locals. Making me promise not to become involved in any arguments, drinking or arm-wrestling competitions, she doles out a note of small denomination and disappears into the *mêlée*.

As a semi-professional in the craft of sniffing out unusual and interesting drinking haunts, I ignore the standard chromium and plate glass-fronted bars around the square and am rewarded after ten minutes of wandering through a network of cobbled alleyways in what is obviously the oldest part of the town. People sometimes accuse me of being more interested in the bars and people who drink in and run them than the local history, industry or architecture, but they do not realise that the best way to learn about any town or city is by calling in at a local pub.

The bar I have found certainly looks as if it has been trading in strong drink and the daily life and dramas of the community for many generations. The fascia is mainly of wood that has clearly not seen a painter's brush for decades, and the satisfyingly incongruous fluted stone pillars on either side of the door are each topped with a carving of a hideously distorted face that would not look out of place as a water spout on the cathedral of Notre Dame. I cannot see inside as the curtains are tight drawn, but the bar has a promising name. For such, as Julius Caesar observed, an imaginative race, the French show remarkably little creative inspiration when naming their pubs. This one is an exception, and rather than a Bar Sporting, Bar Commercial or simply Bar Of The Place, it is called The Bar Of The Good Conversation.

Even in England, not all pubs live up to their names, and when I push my way through the old planking door I find that whatever quality and quantity of conversation had been going on has now stopped. I am clearly the focus of attention for the dozen or so men standing at the bar or seated around the smoke-filled room, and this is obviously not the sort of premises where the owner claims a warm welcome will always be found. Though I am not usually deterred from entering any bar by the appearance or manner of its users, I pause at the doorway and think about leaving. From the Gorbals in Glasgow to the docks area of Marseille, rarely have I been in a pub where the air of hostility is so tangible and the customers so clearly not pleased to see me. I try to look as if I have just remembered a pressing appointment elsewhere, but as I turn away, someone calls my name and I see a familiar and fairly friendly face. It is our village's own international entrepreneur and very dodgy general dealer, Didier Bouvier.

He beckons me over and calls to the barman as I try to walk nonchalantly past a table of men who look as if they are waiting to audition for a re-make of *Night of the Zombies*. We shake hands, and I notice that Didier does not introduce me to his companion, who makes the rest of the clientele look almost effete. He is a tall, strongly-built man with greasily slicked-back dark hair, and was either born with a prognathous jaw or the whole top half of his face has been at some time pushed back beyond its original alignment. During what must have been an interesting life of encounters, his nose has suffered even more collateral damage than mine, a livid scar stretches from beneath one eye to his upper lip, and the puckering of the surrounding skin gives him a permanent but most unfriendly smile. The overall impression of a man you would not wish to meet in even a well-lit alley is enhanced by the selection of crudely-made tattoos on his neck, arms and knuckles. After a cursory inspection, the man pointedly turns his back on me, bangs his glass on the counter and the barman scurries obediently over with a bottle of vodka.

As we wait for our drinks, Didier asks how Donella is getting on with her scrub-burner, then says he has a proposition, and one which could earn me some nice pocket money. This should set warning bells ringing immediately, as Didier's proposals always seem to make money for him and lose money for his partner. But, as usual, I tell myself it will do no harm to at least listen to what he has to say. As someone who uses words for a sort of living, it is a beguiling pleasure to listen to a real master at work. As usual, Didier's proposal is persuasive, and as ever there does not seem to be any catch. In fact, he claims that his idea involves absolutely no investment from me and I will receive a guaranteed and generous cash payment each week for just two hours of my time.

Together with his various other enterprises, Didier explains, he is now to set up a language school. There are hundreds of English people buying homes and moving into our area every year, and all will have regular need of the services of local tradesmen and other service and goods providers. Hardly any of the local people speak a second language except *patois*, and their potential English customers are virtually all free of any knowledge of French. Didier knows that I hold informal classes in French for English newcomers at the Flaming Curtains, and proposes that I now turn my attention to helping local people communicate better with their potential customers. He has so far been to see a variety of craftsmen and shop owners in the area; a surprising number of them have not only shown interest, but signed up for a year's course even after hearing that I would be their teacher. Most people who have met me are aware of my severe limitations in French, Didier says, but this will actually be an asset to the scheme. As well as learning basic English, the students will be getting hands-on experience in communicating with any foreign customers who insist on trying to speak their language. If I am in agreement, the first lesson will take place at the Flaming Curtains early next week, and if I wish, he will actually pay me in advance.

Although, as I reply, we shall have no money problems when we have made a deal with our new publisher and received our substantial advance royalty payment, it would be an interesting project to help the local business community make the most of the influx of English home-buyers and settlers. I would also be very pleased to give something back to an area that has given me and my wife so much. But, I add swiftly, I will accept payment just to put our arrangement on a business footing.

When Didier and I shake hands on the deal and I have

made my usual pleasantry of pretending to count my fingers to see if they are all still there, I empty my glass and try to catch the eye of the barman. He is engaged, and I see that he is methodically re-charging his cigarette stations. Technically, smoking in bars has been prohibited throughout France for almost a decade, but as nobody agrees with the diktat it has gone completely unobserved. Nearly all French barmen I have done business with could smoke for their country, and to some foreign visitors it must seem that having a cigarette dangling precariously from the lips while drawing a drink is a skill requirement of the job. In some busy bars, staff will have a lit cigarette in an ashtray at each end of the counter so they will not be caught short as they shuttle back and forth with orders. This man is taking no chances; like a polar explorer on the outward leg of his expedition, he is carefully leaving supply stations at regular intervals along his route. Together with the emergency rations, the man obviously likes to have back-up facilities in other areas of his life, and is on clearly intimate terms with two women who are standing alone at either end of the bar. One is short and blonde with a low-cut blouse which exposes a pink chasm of a cleavage, and the other dark, tall and willowy. As the barman reaches either end of the bar and completes an order, he will lean across the counter and murmur a few endearments before returning to the neutral zone. My admiration of him only increases when the bead curtain to one side of the bar rattles, and a sharp-faced woman of middle years emerges to pick up a packet of cigarettes from the back of the bar. By the way she talks at him then looks scathingly at each of the women, it is obvious she is his wife. When he finally serves me I ask the man how many cars he owns, but he misses the joke and looks blankly at me before returning to stare with fond affection into the bright eyes and swooping *décolletage* of his blonde friend.

I look at the clock and pay my bill, and Didier walks me to the door. Outside, I follow him round a corner to his pick-up van. As he takes a large holdall bag from the cab I ask about his friend, and Didier casually explains that the man who looks as if he enjoys rat *fricassée* for breakfast is actually the professor of Humanities at a university in the former Yugoslavia. He is visiting Lower Normandy to investigate the possibilities of a twinning arrangement between Cherbourg and Sarajevo, and Didier is merely using his wide circle of contacts with the *beau monde* of the town to help smooth progress.

We shake hands again, and I watch as he re-enters the bar with the holdall. Hearing the bolts shoot, I walk over to the door, gently try the handle then put my eye to a gap between the warped planking. I see that Didier is at the bar busily pulling cardboard cartons from the holdall. Most of the customers have formed a ragged queue, and money is changing hands. As the barman rips open one of the boxes, I realise that I am witnessing the bizarre spectacle of contraband tobacco being sold in a French bar to French smokers. In many British pubs, this would be a common sight, but until recently, tax on tobacco was so low that smokers were prepared to pay the over-the-counter price. But France is many billions of euros in the red, and so the duty on cigarettes has risen dramatically in the past year. As in Britain, the government is trying to take the moral high ground by pretending they are only cranking up the tax to dissuade people from killing themselves, but the inevitable result will be that more and more smokers will buy stolen and thus totally duty-free supplies. It is even being forecast that the French government's next cash-cow target will be wines and spirits. If this happens without a revolution and tax levels eventually overtake those in Britain, it is strange to think that a complete reversal of the normal situation could take place. In the future, we could become used to millions of French people crossing the Channel to eagerly stock up on what they see as cheap tobacco and drink, and there would inevitably be teams of bootleggers making daily runs from Calais to Dover in the French equivalent of an unmarked white Transit van.

*   *   *   *   *

My wife is happily planting the last of the dozen expensive saplings she bought at Sourciéville. I am in the caravan, considering whether bank managers are attracted to the profession because of their nature, or change from Hyde into Jeckyl after regular exposure to an official potion they are required to drink as part of the terms and conditions of their employment agreement. I also wonder if they go on special training courses in how to upset their customers. If there is such a course, I suspect that our local branch at Argenteville is the regional training camp and was probably chosen because we do business there. Seven managers have moved in and out of our lives in recent times, and all have acted as if they were practising their customer-alienating techniques on us.

Reaching the end of his latest letter I realise that our new tormentor is not making a bad joke when he talks of his bank not being an arts foundation with special grants for struggling writers. We have, says Mr Connarde, come to the end of the road. The temporary overdraft we arranged with one of his predecessors three years ago now seems to have become a permanent lease loan, and as we are not registered as a developing country it must be repaid within the next three months. If not, the necessary action will be taken to recover the full sum owing. I think for a moment about calling the bank and asking him why they lent us an umbrella when it was dry, and are demanding its return now that it is raining. I could also ask how Mr Connarde proposes recovering money we do not have, and explain that this is actually the reason we have and need an overdraft. He could, I would say, send a snatch squad to take goods to the sum of our debt, but I doubt if the combined worth of our twenty-year-old Volvo, our scrub-burner, livestock and all our furniture and other possessions would make much of a dent in the sum we owe. We could, I might finally suggest, do a deal committing our famous Cotentin Black chicken to appear in a series of advertisements for his bank. Daisy could even go on a publicity tour of all branches, with me using my past copywriting experience to come up with a suitable slogan for the campaign. Perhaps a snappy line like *Sometimes it does pay to keep all your eggs in one basket* would be a winner.

After thinking up other similarly tart responses I actually compose and write a grovelling letter explaining that we are, as he knows, going through a temporary cashflow crisis but are expecting to receive a significant offer from a major publishing house within the next week. Then, we will be in a position to repay the overdraft in full and have a comfortable sum in our account. I cannot resist adding a subtle sting in the tail by saying how I may even dedicate the new book to him in recognition of all that he had done to keep us afloat till we made our breakthrough. He can be sure that, when the book is an international best-seller, the world will know exactly how he and his bank have treated us.

Feeling a little better, I make coffee and go to see how Donella is getting on with her re-forestation of the roadside copse. I shall not spoil her day by telling her about the letter from Mr Connarde, which I intercepted this morning after my daily vigil at the top of the track waiting for Patrick the Post. Though I usually leave all official correspondence for Donella's attention, our relations with the new manager at Argenteville have become so strained that I have been dealing directly with him. For some reason, this hands-on approach has had the opposite effect to what I hoped would be the outcome. Rather than smoothing things over, I seem to have made the situation worse.

Although I don't like to think about it, the action that the bank would take if the deadline for the repayment of our overdraft is not met would almost certainly be to take our home from us. Our debt is secured by La Puce, and it is not uncommon for banks to repossess a property and sell it off to the highest bidder. Technically, there is a stringent process and code of conduct to ensure that a fair price for a repossessed property is achieved and that there will be money left over for the owners when the bank has received its dues, but this does not always seem to happen. Sometimes, an archaic 'candle sale' auction will be advertised and take place at the property which is to be sold off, with interested parties putting in their bids till the flame dies. Then, details of the highest bid will be placed in local newspapers to see if anyone wishes to top it. Though it may not be true, I have heard that quite often the notices do not appear either before or after the candle sale, and that some properties are sold for a fraction more than the debt that has been secured against them. Often, the buyer will also be someone who is known to the person responsible for organising the sale. Whatever the facts, I know of Britons who have invested all their money, dreams and countless hours of hard work in buying and restoring a home in France, then lost everything when money troubles have arrived. It must be devastating to watch a stranger wander round the home you have given so much time and work to, then see him take it from you with a casually raised finger. This is an experience I could not bear to see my wife endure, and I would do almost anything to stop it happening.

I arrive at the copse and Milly comes streaking through the trees to greet me. Donella is sitting on a tree stump, and I pass her a mug of coffee, put my arm around her shoulder and ask her if she is happy with the planting. She nods contentedly, rests her hand on mine and says it is very satisfying to know that the result of her morning's work will mark our remaining time at La Puce, and that our grandchildren's children may one day be climbing the sturdy trees these small saplings will become.

*   *   *   *   *

I am at the Flaming Curtains to give my first English lesson to members of our local business community. It is nice to know that, for the first time in our long association, I shall be leaving the bar with more money than when I arrived.

As I wait for Didier and my students to arrive, I am sitting at the British Embassy table thinking of how best to structure the course and individual lessons. While I make some hasty notes, Milly is playing football with some local children and Morton the pub dog lies at my feet pretending not to be watching her every move.

English breeds are popular in France, and Morton is a very large and unkempt example of a pedigree Airedale. In some aspects of his character, he is almost as eccentric as his owner, our host at the Flaming Curtains. Although born and raised in this country, there is something of an old-fashioned English gentleman about the way Morton likes to go about his daily routine, and at rest he has the air of a retired army officer taking a post-prandial nap at his club. But Morton's Norman upbringing is evident in his attitude to what he sees as his property and those who trespass on it. Morton views not only the Flaming Curtains as his personal terrain, but also the square and pavement outside. Although he affects a gallic indifference to what is going on around him, he has very strict rules about who he considers welcome to pass through and on to his territory. All male dogs are permanently excluded, and they and their owners obliged to cross the high street if they wish safe passage while passing the *Rideau Cramoisi*. Customers with bitches are welcome, and Morton, like his owner, is regularly surrounded by an admiring audience of females. Unlike his owner, he tends to treat his fan club with an air of indifference and often casual disdain. If in the mood he will acknowledge his favourites, and there is always keen competition to win the favour of a cursory sniff beneath the tail or a passing nod of recognition. But since Milly has become a regular at the Flaming Curtains, things have changed. Morton is obviously smitten with our pretty collie, and she delights in leading him on.

At whatever time I arrive in the square, a giant woolly head will appear at a window or doorway and Morton will bound over to the car and wait to escort Milly inside. As is often the way with relationships between the sexes, the more he pursues and woos her, the more she enjoys keeping him at a distance. The tables have been turned, and now Morton knows the pangs of unrequited love. When Milly is elsewhere, I have often advised him that he should begin to show an overt interest in the pretty spaniel who arrives with her owner most evenings. In my experience of the curious nature of sexual politics, I say, the more attention he pays to her the more chance he will have of gaining Milly's interest. I think he has taken note of my suggestions, and I have seen him make several awkward attempts at small talk with the spaniel. But Milly is a collie, and obviously far too clever to be taken in by this clumsy male ploy.

*   *   *   *   *

I have taken my first English language class and, all things considered, it seemed to go well. Some of the local traders were clearly more interested in numeracy than literacy. The craftsmen were particularly interested in how best to say to their English clients that the work would take much longer than anticipated and would therefore cost considerably more. They were also surprised to learn that their traditional sharp intake of breath and shake of head when surveying a proposed job is as common in Britain as it is in France.

Peculiarly, among the local students were a handful of strangers who seemed to be as unfamiliar with their own language as they were with mine. When I asked Didier about them, he said that they were country people from the Basque region and not used to speaking proper French. They were planning to move to this area and find work, and so would benefit from the classes by getting to know the local people while learning English and reminding themselves of how the rest of France communicated. I have never met any Basques and did not realise how different and guttural their language sounds, but can understand the problems and frustrations of not being able to speak properly with people from even your own country. Perhaps I shall introduce them to my new friend from Newcastle and see if he can give them any tips.

After handing over my fee, Didier said that although he knew I did not need the money, there was another job I might like to do for him. Now that the English courses were established, he would like to move on to the next phase of the project, which was to organise educational and leisure visits to Britain for some of his clients. This application of the system of French students spending some time with a typical English family and learning about their home life and culture would be invaluable to some members of our class, he said. Another bonus would be that the craftsmen would be able to study the favoured building techniques in England, and by eating with the family, might even develop a tolerance for English food and cooking that would stand them in good stead if invited to dinner by their clients in Lower Normandy. He knew that I would have the names and addresses of many readers who had written to say how much they had enjoyed my books, and he would pay me a good price for every one I contacted and introduced to the scheme as a host family. They too would gain much from the experience as they would get to know the real people who actually live in our area of France. I said it seemed a good idea, and would contact and put the idea to some of my readers. I like the thought of them meeting some of the characters I write about, but have insisted that the name of

110

René Ribet will not appear on the list of Didier's proposed foreign placement students.

*   *   *   *   *

The end of a pleasant night by the fire. I have given what is left of my tuition fee to Donella after the cost of the round or two of drinks I stood in the bar, and the bouquet of flowers I bought at St. Sauveur. In return for the unexpected contribution to the housekeeping budget and the even more unexpected gift, my wife let me win the nightly round of killer dominoes and opened a bottle of our special reserve sparkling nettle wine. Not only does last autumn's brewing have a pleasant flavour, but it is particularly satisfying to gain revenge on an old enemy by first boiling him alive and then drinking his juices.

And so we sit in the comfort of our home and all seems well in our small world. Our old apple-wood clock sporadically chimes to mark the passing hours, the rain drums on the window in frustration, and the dancing flames from the woodburning stove cast flickering shadows across the undulating whitewashed walls. Donella is working on a tapestry for the hen-house, Milly is curled at my feet, and we are making plans for the future. When our offer from the publisher comes through, I say, we will have enough money to pay off our overdraft and to finally restore the ruined end of the mill cottage. I have also thought of a refinement to Didier's student placement scheme. Earlier this evening, I phoned or sent e-mail messages to several British readers and three have already said they would be interested in accommodating one or more of my students. When the system is up and running and the extra rooms have been built here, I propose that we offer our hosts and perhaps all our readers what I shall call

The Mill of the Flea Experience. For much less than the price of renting an anonymous gîte, they will be able to stay with us and discover what it is like to live here. We can take them on guided tours of the area and meet the people who feature in my books. As I have said so many times before, money makes money and it is easy to action good ideas when you have some.

Donella leaves off her needlework representation of Daisy's triumph at the Cotentin chicken show, looks at me over the top of her glasses and reminds me that I have had this idea before. As she said then, it has several drawbacks. The first consideration is that I do not like having visitors, and it would not be fair on them to see me parading around the cottage at all hours in my underwear. Also, finding out what life is really like at the Mill of the Flea may not be the sort of experience for which most people would wish to pay.

I accept that the nettle wine has probably clouded my judgement, and agree that she is probably right. In any case, as soon as we have secured a good deal with our publisher, the last thing we shall need to worry about is extra income.

*   *   *   *   *

Milly and I are taking a late-night stroll around our land. I need to walk off the effects of the nettle champagne, and my mind is full of thoughts of how the events of the next few days could change our lives. The publishing company's board meeting takes place tomorrow, and it will be hard to resist phoning the director and asking him how his proposal was received. I know I should wait for his letter, but perhaps I will ask Donella to call his secretary and ask if she knows what happened at the meeting.

As I think about the way our lives are shaped by other people and by events over which we seem to have little control, Milly stops in her tracks and lifts her head to scent the night air. So far, our moonlight ramble has taken us round the big pond, through the copse and down the bank to the river and along its winding length to the back of the cottage. It is a quiet night and we have not seen or heard anything unusual, but Milly has detected something happening by the chicken coop. I signal for her to stay, then get to my knees and crawl towards the enclosure. Perhaps it is only a prowling fox, or perhaps the visitor with an interest in our celebrity chicken has two legs. As I draw nearer, I hear the sound of rustling and muted squawking, so pick up a fallen branch and launch myself around the corner of the compound.

Instead of intruders, I see that I have caught our unfaithful hen in the act of betraying her partner. Daisy and Fred have obviously slipped away from their marital beds to make the two-backed beast behind the manure pile. They are so engrossed in each other that they do not see me, and feeling uncomfortably like a voyeur I withdraw, whistle softly to Milly, and sneak away.

*　　　*　　　*　　　*　　　*

The day of the board meeting, and I have made an early start. I have already gathered enough wood to see us through until autumn, taken an early breakfast at the big pond with Hen the duck, and fed the chickens. When I topped up their food dispensers and cleaned their quarters out, Fred avoided eye contact and Daisy brazenly stared me out, so perhaps they know I was a witness to their late-night coupling. There was also a strained atmosphere in both their apartments, so I think their partners must suspect what is going on.

To keep myself occupied until it is a respectable time for Donella to call the publishing house in London, I intend working off my nervous energy on our land. After setting fire to one of the tool sheds while I was practising with the new scrub-burner, I am not allowed to use it without supervision so am going to employ more traditional methods to attack the bramble patch by the big pond. In fact, the bramble patch by the big pond is now mostly in the big pond. From what I have read about *rubus fruticosus* it cannot survive under water, but our variety has obviously not read the same book. The newest patch marched relentlessly across the water meadow throughout last summer, and its tentacles now snake down the bank and below the surface of the pond. Although it is supposed to be a strictly vegetarian plant, I think it may have developed a taste for protein from our bloody encounters and has now decided to try fishing for additional nourishment.

An hour has passed when I sense a presence and look up from my work to see Mr Trefle regarding me with his usual expression of pained incredulity. He asks me why I am attacking my pond, and when I explain that I am lopping off the tentacles of a fish-eating bramble patch, he nods, looks warily at my sickle and takes a step back. I ask him what he wants, and he says my wife called to tell him that one of his steers has escaped and is loose on our land. I agree to help him round the animal up, and as he turns away I lob a large stone into the water. He turns at the sound of the splash, and I grab his arm and warn him to get no closer. As he shrugs free I say I am sure he will know that there is nothing more dangerous than a wounded and enraged bramble plant, and a nosy local who ignored my warning and got too close to the water's edge last week has not been seen or heard of since. I am sure my little game will not put him off snooping on our land, but it made me feel better and will give him yet another story to tell his cronies.

*　　　*　　　*　　　*　　　*

I have heard people who live in urban areas say that nothing much happens in the countryside, and that they would be bored just watching grass grow. They do not realise how much time is taken up dealing with apparently trivial events and their consequences in a rural setting.

For the past three hours, we have been chasing Mr Trefle's steer around La Puce. Together with breaking three flower pots, several panes of glass in the greenhouse and doing serious damage to the vegetable garden, the frightened animal has also left its mark on the terrace and all along the track up to the road. Ironically, the only place it did not deposit any of the contents of its stomach was on the vegetable garden, where at least it would have done some good. I also sprained my wrist badly when attempting to wrestle the creature to the ground by its horns. The technique works well in movies about the Old West, but is not as easy in practice as it appears on film.

To add insult to all the physical injury, I have had a stand-up row with Mr Trefle. Rather than apologising for the damage caused by his steer, he blamed our lack of skills in helping capture it and even threatened to sue me if the beast has suffered any physical hurt or mental trauma. He says that our clumsy attempts to catch it caused his valuable and sensitive animal to panic, and it was anyway our fault it got out of his field. He claimed that under Norman law, I had a duty to help maintain the rotten fence running alongside the boundary with his field and it was my side that gave way when the steer charged it. Although I have seen how Mr Trefle treats his animals and his claims are patent nonsense, I have had enough experience of how the law is applied in any dispute between a local landowner and a foreigner to think about taking him on in court. As if all these distractions on such an important day were not enough, when the steer was finally back in its paddock and I had repaired the broken fence, Mr Trefle's old car would not start. He is now sulking in the mill cottage until his son arrives with the family tractor and a tow-rope, and we are marooned as his car is blocking the track. My only consolation is that he has been helping himself to our nettle champagne while he waits, and I know how he will feel when he sobers up.

Now that a sort of peace has descended on La Puce, I have retreated to the caravan to wait for news from London. During our dramas with the steer, Donella called the publishing director's secretary every hour and we know that the board meeting which will decide our future is still in session. The secretary says that the meeting has been going on for much longer than usual, and although she should not tell us company business, she knows it has been a lively one. She added that there are several manuscripts being proposed for major publication this autumn, and there has been disagreement on which ones to choose. She sounds like a kind woman and obviously appreciates how we must feel, and has promised to call us with any news as soon as she hears it. If her boss asks her to send us a letter, she will let us know what it says before she posts it. While Donella entertains Mr Trefle and waits for any call, I have decided to deal with my electronic correspondence. I pull the curtains, switch on my portable computer and prepare to go on-line.

Although I am by nature and age opposed to those advances in technology which require us to spend time and money doing things we don't really need to do, I have found the electronic superhighway of communications a generally useful and interesting road to travel. At the touch of a button and at hardly any cost, I can receive and send messages to and from anywhere in the world. Apart from the advantages of being able to find out if it is raining in Tokyo and what someone in Okefenokee is having for lunch, I like the feeling of being able to talk with and travel the rest of the planet while sitting in a leaky caravan in a field in Lower Normandy. It is said that the telephone killed off the practice and art of letter writing, but it seems to me that electronic mail has revived it, and this can only be for the good.

The screen glows, the connections are made, and a series of messages appear on the screen. Looking at the addresses of the senders, I see I have news from friends and readers in California, South Africa and Pudsey. There is also a handful of unfamiliar names and call signs which will introduce new Friends of the Flea wanting to share with me their plans and dreams and schemes for buying a home in France and perhaps one day moving over the Channel to start a new life.

*   *   *   *   *

It has been an absorbing hour. Apart from news from regular correspondents, I have made several new friends and been able to give some practical advice. Although we are still strangers, most of the people who contact me on this subject end by asking whether I think they will be happy and successful if they take the big step across the Channel. It is flattering that they should ask my opinion, but I am always non-committal. It would be hard if I thought that I had encouraged people to do something which might not turn out well for them. In reply to these enquiries, I usually say that, apart from not knowing the people making them, it anyway seems to me to be impossible to define the sort of character best suited to living in a foreign land. I have, however, noticed that British expatriates seem to fall into three broad categories.

One is made up of those types who become curiously more British the longer they stay in another country. They develop a nostalgic longing for things they often took for granted at home, and can become quite obsessive about reminders of what they left behind. In our area, I know of one couple who regularly drive to the ferry-port at Cherbourg to watch cars with British number plates coming out of the gates.

The second category contains the Britons who wish to

117

become totally absorbed into the culture of the country in which they have chosen to live. In extreme cases, they go native and go to great lengths to break any links with their heritage and past. They will actively avoid any British visitors or fellow settlers, and if approached by them will often pretend to be French and unable to speak a word of English.

The third general category includes those who have no wish to disassociate themselves from their upbringing and culture, but who are able and willing to adapt to their new circumstances and surroundings. They will always be foreigners, and will strive to understand and accept that, like the past, where they have chosen to make their home is a foreign country and things are often done differently there.

Of those broad groups, people within this category seem to be the most content with their new lives in France, and I like to think my wife and I fit, however awkwardly, into it.

Sometimes though, even the most adaptable types can encounter problems in whichever country they wish to settle. A classic if extreme example amongst my e-messages today was from an American reader who said she was inspired by my books to buy a holiday and retirement home in Brittany, and she was particularly enthused because she thought even she could not possibly make as many errors of judgement as me.

With her second home a little over seven thousand miles from her front door in California and a scant knowledge of Breton-French, the lady found and commissioned a British builder to conduct or oversee every stage of the restoration of her impressive but dilapidated 19th-century townhouse. After setting up a bank account in Brittany and giving him access to it, she arrived a month later to find no work done on the house and her account empty. The rogue builder had obviously gone off in search of his next victim. Determined not to make the same mistake again, the lady decided to employ a local builder. To be doubly sure, she also appointed a local businesswoman to manage the project and keep a watchful eye on the builder. Hearing nothing from and unable to contact the woman after the initial progress reports, she took another unplanned flight to France. Arriving at the village, she learned that the prolonged and intimate contact between her builder and his minder had flowered into romance, and the couple had run off and left their families to start a new life elsewhere.

Now, said my correspondent, she has decided to take a hands-on approach to the situation and is staying in France until her future home is totally restored. She has found a third and this time totally honest and reliable builder, but there have been some teething troubles because of the inevitable communication problems. On their first inspection tour she had told him that she wanted virtually every piece of worm-ridden wood in the house removed, with the exception of the striking and elaborately panelled staircase that wound its way down to the lobby. When she arrived at the house the next day she was pleased to find that the builder had made an early start. She was much less pleased to see that he had left all the rotten and ugly post-war fixtures and fittings in place, but had dismantled and destroyed the classic staircase.

My last message today embodied a reminder that the old legal caution of *caveat emptor* is wise advice wherever you choose to set up home. It came from a Scotsman who has lived in the Midi for two years after buying and restoring a derelict property which was once part of a large farm. At the time of purchase, he and his wife decided not to accept the farmer's suggestion that they also buy an adjoining field at what was a very reasonable price. Having turned the former cowshed into a magnificent, five-bedroomed property, he asked the farmer if he could now buy a small corner of the neighbouring field for additional parking space. The farmer said he would think about it, then returned a month later with his proposal. The whole field was certainly available for purchase, he said, and the price would be the equivalent of twenty thousand pounds. When he had recovered, my correspondent asked how such an isolated and unproductive patch of land could be worth such a price. Without a blink, the farmer explained that since they had last met he had applied for and gained planning permission on the field. It was now a valuable piece of real estate, and if my correspondent did not wish to buy it, he was sure that he could find a builder who would like to create a nice little housing estate there.

*   *   *   *   *

My electronic letters answered, I draw the curtains and wave encouragingly to Hen the duck, who is helping with my pond-clearing efforts by launching a series of underwater attacks on the bramble tentacles. As I turn to switch it off, the computer emits an urgent bleep, and a new message flashes up on the screen. I put on my glasses, and see from the sender's address that it comes from the London offices of the publishing company. I walk around the caravan, roll and light two cigarettes, run my hand through my hair, sit down and stand up several times, cross and uncross my fingers and legs, then reach out and tentatively touch the button to reveal the message which may change our lives.

Part Two

He that wants money, means and content is without three good friends.

William Shakespeare, *As You Like It.*

April

The swallows have returned to La Puce, so summer is on the wing. Of all species, I think I like and admire these tenacious and energetic little birds the most. When I am low, it lifts my heart to sit and watch them swooping and wheeling joyously above the pond and making the most of their time with us. It is said they spend every moment of their short lives in the air, and sometimes I wish that I could join them and be as free from concern as they seem. Like us though, I am sure they have their own worries.

It is early morning and I have slept badly. The black dog of depression is a rare visitor to our home, but he has been my constant companion for more than a week. When I had not appeared at the cottage by dusk on the day we heard from the publishing company, Donella came to look for me. She found me sitting beside the Hobbit tree, and when she asked me what was wrong I told her about the message. It was apologetic, I said, but short and to the point and said that the board had decided not to make a major investment in publishing and promoting my new book. In fact, they had decided not to make any investment in my work. In a curious application of logic, the publishing director said that he thought that my book was too good to be published in a small way, so they would not be making me an offer to publish it in any way.

Because she is who she is, my wife refused to let me wallow in self-pity, and became angry when I said we should stop struggling against fate and give up trying to make a living from my writing. When I said I was going to burn all copies of the manuscript for our new book and write off the last thirty years and look for a proper job, she said I should stop acting like a spoilt child who can't have what he wants. She could name a hundred writers and artists who struggled all their lives, experienced dreadful poverty and did not become well-known until long after they died. Besides, who did I think was going to give me a real job? The only person I had worked for in the past twenty years was myself, and that was rarely a smooth working relationship. She then reminded me that the reason I became self-employed all those years ago was because I am basically unemployable. What else did I think I could or would do rather than write?

I replied that I knew - or hoped - that she was trying to cheer me up, but that I would much rather have greater recognition and the consequent rewards while I was still around to enjoy them. It is a matter of record that many great writers were not recognised until they were dead, but being unrecognised does not mean that I am a great or even a good writer. It could just be that I have been fooling myself all these years, and nobody wants to hear what I have to say.

Also, we might not be living in poverty, but she did not realise just how serious our money problems were. When I began to tell her about the latest letter from Mr Connarde, she said she knew all about it and had been corresponding with him for weeks without my knowledge as managing money was far too important a subject to be left to me. She had spoken to our bank manager earlier that day, and he had agreed to extend the deadline for settling our overdraft by another month. That would at least give us more time to come up with the money. I refused to be optimistic, and said that if we had another year of grace we would not be able to raise such a large sum. Without telling her, I had already talked to the other major banks in the region to see if they would lend us the money to pay off Mr Connarde, but all had turned me down. One manager even said he had heard all about me, and he and his company thought it was a good idea for me to keep our account exactly where it was, with their main banking rival. We are, I said, in a classic *Catch-22* situation. The advance royalties on the new book would have solved all our money problems, but now we have no publisher. We cannot bring the new book out ourselves as we do not have the money that we would have had if someone else had published it.

I have also shut our last remaining escape hatch from the wrong side. Immediately after getting the message from London, I had called the director of the travel book company and said we had changed our minds about his offer and we would accept any level of publication and promotion of my new work. He was sympathetic, but said I was too late. When he learned I was not interested, his company had looked elsewhere for a new author to take on, and had now allocated their publishing budget for the year.

With no income to come from the new book, I said, we had finally reached the end of a dead-end road. In three months, the bank would repossess La Puce, and we could lose nearly everything. With the boom in property prices in Britain, we would not be able to afford even a one-bedroomed flat there, and would probably end up living in a council house if we were lucky.

I have read about people snorting in derision, but before our exchange I had not heard anyone making that specific noise. After giving a good impression of a horse with a novice and very stupid rider on its back, my wife told me to pull myself together and said that I had no excuse for being so morbid and histrionic, especially as I had not been drinking. There was an obvious solution to our financial problems, and one which we had discussed before when times had been especially tight.

We would just have to sell La Puce. Rather than let the bank take and dispose of our home at a knock-down price, we should put our home on the market and get the best price for it. Although not on a level with Britain, property prices have been steadily rising in Lower Normandy. If we were to sell La Puce, we would easily be able to settle all our debts and still have enough money to buy a new home. It would not be anything like La Puce, but as long as there was enough room for us and our animals we could make it a home. If we were to set ourselves a budget and find a real bargain, we would also have enough money to publish my new book in a big way. Instead of depending on the whims of the established publishing companies and expecting them to risk their money, we should show our belief in my work by risking our own. Then, when my work was at the top of the best-seller lists, we would have enough money to buy a bigger, better place to live. We could even buy La Puce back, whatever the new owners set the price at. Most importantly, my new book would be published, and I would be able to keep on writing. She knew that there was nothing else I wanted to do with my life, and whatever it cost, we must follow my heart. Besides, to stop now would be a waste of half a lifetime of struggle. Even if success did not come until after my death, she would hopefully still be around to enjoy the benefits.

*   *   *   *   *

Donella is cooking our evening meal, and I am sitting by the cascade. I went into the cottage earlier and saw that she had been crying. When I said I hated myself for what was happening and for making her so unhappy, she told me not to be stupid and that she was crying because she had been peeling an onion. It was not a good excuse as I know we are having egg and chips for supper, but I loved her even more for making it.

*   *   *   *   *

I have agreed that we will go through the motions of putting La Puce on the market, but I really cannot imagine us actually leaving our home. I have also told Mr Connarde what is happening, and he sounded quite unhappy. I think he regrets being the cause of us selling our home, but Donella thinks he is just annoyed that his bank will not be able to sell it to someone they know at a knock-down price.

Although we are seeing a local property agent tomorrow, I still believe that something fortuitous may happen between now and the deadline. We have been in tight corners before and something has always turned up, and since Donella helped me chase the black dog away I am in a very positive mood. Yesterday, I bought twenty tickets in the national lottery and I have been investigating all sorts of money-making schemes advertised on the Internet. According to some of the claims, it is possible to make thousands of pounds a week in return for a few moments work and a very small investment. I do not think I am particularly credulous, and know that the only people making money out of most of the proposals are the individuals and companies who are making them. But there may be some genuine business opportunities amongst the junk mail, and I shall be very selective before taking any risks with money we do not have.

Although we need such a large amount to pay off Mr Connarde, I must also be sure not to neglect any opportunities to bring in less spectacular sums, and I think my partnership with Didier in the foreign exchange scheme could be quite rewarding. Before this evening's lesson, he told me that my Basque students had been so pleased with my tuition and the foreign placement scheme that they had asked to continue their studies by going to stay with a family in Britain. I would now be due a commission fee for providing the introduction to the hosts. Even better news was that the Basque contingent had told their friends at home how pleased they were with the scheme, and another six students from a village near the border with Spain would be joining us for the evening's lesson.

After our session in the upstairs room, I invited the students to join me in the bar and tried to give them a practical demonstration of the rules of engagement in a typical British public house. I think they enjoyed the session, but, like nearly all my French friends, had real difficulty in understanding the idea of taking it in turns to buy rounds and paying with the order rather than at the end of the evening.

During the evening, I also met Jean-Claude Goulot's latest female companion, though I learned she is not a customer of his one-man escort agency business. A statuesque blonde from Essex, Kara told me she met Jean-Claude at a Cherbourg 70s revival disco evening, and was impressed by the authenticity of his period clothing. When she learned he wears his suit of lights all the time, she realised he had need of her services. Kara is unusual in that she has two areas of expertise and income; during the day she works as a relationships counsellor, and by night as one half of a pole-dancing duo billed as Twin Cheeks. The pun does not work at all when translated into French on the posters outside the night clubs where they are appearing, but as she said, the punters get the message from the photographs. Now, she has agreed to act as Jean-Claude's lifestyle coach and mentor, and may become a partner in his escort agency business. Amongst other achievements, Kara, which she insists is her real name, claims to have been married three times, had any number of nervous breakdowns, and has even tried to commit suicide. When I asked her if she thought this was a good track record for someone who charges people for telling them how to live their lives, she said that was the whole point. Because she has been through all those emotional traumas, she is ideally equipped to guide others through their pain and suffering. She is totally in touch with her own feelings and will, she said, always be there for Jean-Claude. When I asked exactly what she meant by 'there' and whether that place would be in the Flaming Curtains or up a pole at one of her venues, she looked at me as if unsure whether I was being facetious, then asked if I had thought about taking on a life coach, as she had never met anyone more obviously in need of one. Together she and my ex-carpenter friend make a singular and somehow sad couple, but seem comfortable together and I think the combination of their talents and assets may work well in some bars and clubs in Cherbourg's bohemian quarter.

*   *   *   *   *

It is good to have real friends.

Before he closed the bar, Coco invited me to stay on for a night-cap and when the last customer had left we settled down at the bar with a bottle of his good wine and the distributor head from his Land Rover. After we had adjusted the gap and smoked and drunk and talked about nothing, he said he had heard that I was thinking of selling La Puce. As I had only talked about the sale with Mr Connarde and our English agent, this was more evidence that our area's communications system is at least as efficient as the Internet. When I said it was true we were considering moving on to somewhere smaller and more manageable, Coco remarked that, as the local expression has it, one should never try to blow smoke up a bull's backside. He knew that we had money problems, and this was nothing to be ashamed of. I was an artist, and he would somehow think less of me if I had learned the trick of popularising and making real money from my work. He did not wish to embarrass me or spoil our friendship, but he and Chantal had a small amount they were saving for retirement. If it would help, I would be welcome to the money and could pay him back when things got better. I looked at my friend and wondered how many local people he has quietly helped over the years, then thanked him for his offer and refused it. After he had opened another bottle and we had talked some more, he came up with a compromise. From now on, I would pay for all my drinks at the Flaming Curtains with copies of my books, valued at the cover price. He would sell them to English visitors at an advantageous conversion rate into euros, and we would both make a profit from the arrangement. As he said, it was unlikely that the savings on my weekly bar bill would be enough to pay off our overdraft within the next three months, but given my rate of consumption it would surely make a healthy dent in it.

*   *   *   *   *

We are visiting a friend's home to talk about the sale of La Puce and start the search for a new home in Lower Normandy.

At the Château Epinguet, we find the owner looking bemusedly at a small mountain of septic tanks on his driveway. To visitors, the collection of large plastic boxes might seem at odds with the imposing façade of the great house and its landscaped gardens. To us and those who know Mark, the serried ranks of waste disposal units are just a sign that it is business as usual.

Although he occasionally seems to be living in another dimension, Mark is one of the most decent and genuine men I know. Being also adaptable, durable and more than a little what some people might call eccentric, he is also ideally suited to living in Lower Normandy and helping other people find property here. His experiences have also developed the sense of humour which is a vital commodity in his line of business anywhere, and especially in France. Having moved to the Cotentin and set up as a property agent fifteen years ago, Mark is a veteran at dealing with his British customers and the owners of the property they wish to buy. He has also become adept at dealing with the regulations and authorities whose job it is to make property transfer as awkward and time-consuming as possible. It was Mark who helped us find and buy La Puce, and it seems fitting that it is to him we come to talk about the possibility of selling our home and finding a new one.

With his wife Fiona, Mark runs what is almost a one-stop-shopping service from their home. Those in search of property in the area can stay at the *château*, be taken on tours of available properties in their price range and then nursed through the buying process. They can also take advantage of Mark's experience and contacts throughout the region after they have bought their home in the Cotentin, which explains why the mountain of septic tanks is currently blocking the driveway to his stately home.

Having negotiated the *fosse-septique* chicane, we are invited into the private quarters and take a seat under the boar's head which is mounted on the wall and for some reason has been named George. When we explain our situation, Mark appears crestfallen. He knows how happy we have been at La Puce, but understands our reasons for having to put the cottage, farmhouse and grounds on the market. When we have taken a glass of wine and talked about what has been happening in our lives and areas, Mark says he is sure he can find us a buyer for La Puce. It is, he says politely, a most unusual property, but over the years he has found there is always a customer for every house, wherever it is and whatever condition it is in. I can see that Mark will enjoy taking on the challenge of finding that customer. Like us, his personal tastes in property are unusual, and he is at his happiest when finding and selling a dilapidated *manoir*, distressed mill or completely ruined castle.

When we have agreed on what seems a fair price for La Puce, we climb over the pile of septic tanks, and while Donella goes to speak to Fiona I confess to Mark that I may be wasting his time. I have only agreed that we should sell La Puce because I know my wife is concerned about our overdraft and is also determined that my new book be published. I know that, whatever she says, it would break her heart to have to leave our home and I intend to do everything I can to stop that happening.

As my wife approaches, Mark says he understands and that he would probably feel the same. He will do his best to find us a buyer and another property at a bargain price, and if it will help he will forego his commission on the sale. But knowing how much we love La Puce, he will be more than happy if his efforts to sell it are wasted.

As we shake hands, Mark asks if we would like a sale board put up on the roadside at La Puce. I look quickly at my wife's face and say that we would not like to advertise the fact that we are moving, and Mark agrees that it would only start rumours about our financial situation circulating in the area. Actually, he will know that there will be few local people who do not already know that La Puce is for sale and why, but he also understands what that sign would mean to my wife. Before we get into the car, Donella turns back to Mark and says in a small voice that he must, of course, accept an offer from anyone who comes up with the asking price, but it would be nice if they were the sort of people who he thinks would love and look after our old home and be as happy there as we have been. Our friend nods and kisses her cheek, and as we drive off, I see that he has taken out a handkerchief and is pretending to blow his nose. It is good to know that despite their reputation, some estate agents, unlike most bank managers, have a soul.

*   *   *   *   *

As if my poor wife did not have enough to worry about, my fears that Cato is fighting his last fight may be well founded. Without telling Donella, I took our cat to the vet at La Haye-du-Puits this morning, and he says that Cato has stomach cancer. He is an honest and good man who obviously cares deeply for all the animals he treats, and told me that there is little he or we can do. He said there was a very expensive course of treatment, but all he thought it could do was delay the inevitable. I paid for the box of powder anyway, and promised him I would not let Cato suffer by avoiding our duty when the time came to give her her final freedom from pain. I will add the medicine to Cato's food when Donella is not there to see me, and not tell her the result of the tests. I am sure she knows what is happening to her beloved cat, but it must be best for her to live in hope for a little longer.

*   *   *   *   *

It has been a long and disappointing day.

In spite of my determination that we shall not have to sell La Puce, I had been looking forward to our first viewing trip. Though we have had no reason to consider buying another property in France for more than a decade, I still find it almost impossible to pass an estate agency. As some women are drawn to clothing, shoe or cake shops, I cannot resist pressing my nose against any window through which I can see property details. In our area, I have become such a familiar sight outside some agencies that the staff now either ignore me, or wave and smile as if to an old friend. Some even invite me in for a coffee and chat though they know I am not a potential customer.

I am also always eager to hear about other people's interest in owning a home in France. Every year, I receive hundreds of letters and e-mails from readers telling me about their plans to buy, and I love to keep them company as they travel through the various stages of initial excitement and optimism, disappointment, frustration, fear and then hopeful fulfilment. While many people stifle a yawn, change the subject or even feign a heart attack to avoid hearing the latest bulletin about their friends' property across the Channel, I actually ask to see the photographs. Today, though, we have not seen a single property to get in the least excited about.

When we began looking for a home in Normandy, the region appeared to be overflowing with characterful old properties just waiting for their potential to be unlocked. Every visit to an isolated hamlet, village or town was a journey of anticipation, and what lay hidden at the end of a pot-holed track was often a treasure. During our journeying around the peninsula we saw once-grand *manoirs*, decaying yet enchanting cottages and deserted farmhouses still alive with the echoes of their past. All were waiting patiently for someone to arrive and bring them to life again, and some of the prices made it seem that we had travelled back in time as well as across the English Channel. But today has shown us much evidence of how times change.

Perhaps it is because we are now older and just a little wiser, and have learned through experience the true cost in time and money of restoring a ruined property. Perhaps because it is now likely that we shall need to find and buy a new home, we were looking with clearer and more calculating eyes at the properties for sale. For whatever reason, our journeying ended in disappointment and sometimes even disbelief. Every property we saw was uninspiring and most seemed, by French standards, grossly over-priced. We had thought that Mark's valuation of La Puce was optimistic, but now realise just how much property prices in Normandy have risen in recent years.

During our journey, we looked at derelict and unappetising cottages with little or no land for sale at twice the value we would have placed upon them. We also saw empty properties which had obviously been commercially restored and dressed for sale, even down to a pile of artistically arranged logs next to the unused stove. For the first time since moving to Lower Normandy, we were seeing homes which had obviously been bought and renovated and converted for no other purpose than to sell at a profit. With what the French have started to call *l'invasion* of buyers from other parts of Europe, this should not be an unexpected development, but it was somehow sad to see the evidence that property speculation will inevitably play a large part in the economic future of our region. However unlikely it may have seemed a few years ago, it is possible that the French will now become as obsessed as the British with the value of their homes. Until recently, people in our towns and villages mostly looked on a house as somewhere to live and raise the family. When they died, the family home would be passed on to the next generation. Lives and futures were not governed by how much you had paid for your house and how much it might be worth now. From what we have seen today, it seems that this traditional attitude may change dramatically. Homes will inevitably become valuable commodities, and the character of the rural landscape and the sort of people who live there will change, just as it has in Britain.

When we stopped at a bar and I voiced my fears to Donella, she said that I sounded just like the English NIMACS in the Bar Ghislaine. Times change, and we could not expect our little part of France to remain the same forever. I should not condemn other foreigners for wanting to do what we did, or local people and places to stay unchanged just to suit my romantic notions. And if I was looking for someone to blame, she reminded me, I must bear a tiny fraction of the responsibility as I have spent the last ten years telling people how wonderful life can be in the French countryside.

My wife is probably right, but I still feel saddened to think that, by their desire to be part of all that has been so unchanging about rural France, the very people who so admire it will be those who help to destroy it. On a practical note, what

135

we have seen today could mean that our chances of finding an interesting old property at a good price are, to say the least, remote.

* * * * *

More tales of the unexpected in the mail today, and our postman had a decidedly different look about him. As he rolled down the track, I saw that Patrick was sporting a new uniform and trendy high-heeled boots and had neglected to wear his official crash-helmet. He was smoking a long cheroot rather than his perennial roll-up cigarette, and his normally lank and mousy hair was standing to attention in rigid black tufts. When I asked him if he had forgotten his helmet and if his hair was standing on end because one of his customers had asked for a loan, he gave me a condescending look and said it was obvious that I was completely out of touch with modern fashion. His hairstyle was all the rage in Paris, and he was not going to spoil it by wearing an ugly non-designer helmet. Besides, helmets were for women and sissies. Life was for living, and a whiff of danger added to a man's appeal. Coming from someone who wears a surgical mask to deliver his letters to our doctor's surgery, this new attitude to risk-taking was as much of a surprise as his sudden attack of fashion-consciousness. After handing over my package of mail and refusing my offer of breakfast, he said that his recent trip to Paris had opened his eyes to a whole new world, and to the fact that life was not a rehearsal. He added that he also had Didier Bouvier to thank for his transformation, and took out and showed me a small bottle of what looked like cough medicine. It was, he said, a very expensive vitality tonic, but worth every euro. Since he had started taking it, he had become a new man and was now determined to make up for lost time. The most amazing thing about the potion was how well it worked below the belt. Such was his potency now that even his wife had begun to complain of headaches at bedtime, and was talking about moving in to the spare room. With that, he winked broadly and said he would not be staying for breakfast as he had a large package to give to the Widow of Négreville and knew she was anxious to get it. After attempting a wheelie on his moped in our turning circle he shouted out that I should try a bottle of Didier's elixir, as with all the beer I drank I would otherwise soon be needing a pair of splints to perform my marital duties.

After I watched our dramatically revitalised postman gunning his *mobylette* up the track and straight out on to the road to a chorus of squealing brakes and lorry horns, I opened the day's post and learned I may be able to help avoid a serious international diplomatic incident.

Amongst the bulky envelopes of property details from agents who have obviously heard about our situation, there was a letter containing a plea from a reader who lives in the picturesque and normally tranquil Dorset village of Corfe Castle. My correspondent explained that, some years ago, his village received a visit from the then mayor of our nearest town. The purpose was to discuss the twinning of Corfe with St. Sauveur-le-Vicomte. The idea was mooted because, if having little else in common, both places boast a ruined castle. After several days of earnest discussions and civic junketing, the mayor of St. Sauveur was presented with a souvenir in the form of a cannon ball which may or may not have been fired in anger at or from Corfe Castle. As is the way of these things in France, time slipped by after the mayor of St. Sauveur returned to his day job as an ironmonger and nothing more was heard of the twinning idea. Now, I read, the Corfe sub-committee set up to administer the project wants its ball back.

Knowing about my connections with St. Sauveur, my correspondent proposes I try and locate the cannon ball and reclaim it for its original owners. My reward, if successful, will be a large bottle of champagne. The committee will also be happy to pay the postage on the missile, which they realise may be costly because of its weight. There is even talk of granting me the freedom of the village if I bring their ball back in person.

I shall write and say that I am honoured to be offered this opportunity to prevent a possible rift in the *entente-cordiale* between the two locations. I shall add that I will visit the castle at St. Sauveur on my way to the Flaming Curtains today, but I do not hold out much hope of success for my mission. If it is there, I will clearly have a problem in identifying the English ball amongst the dozens on show at the castle, and, given the occupation of the former mayor, there is always the chance he may have absent-mindedly had it melted down for its scrap value.

*   *   *   *   *

Another day of driving around the peninsula looking at unsuitable properties. The deadline for repaying our overdraft approaches inexorably, and I have not been able to come up with a scheme to save us from having to sell La Puce. I am now becoming almost resigned to moving to a smaller, cheaper property so that we will be able to settle our debts and pay for the publication of my new book. Our problem is obviously going to be finding any sort of reasonable new home at the price we can afford to pay. We shall probably have to move to an area where most people do not wish to live and houses are cheap, even for rural France. Although prices are still a fraction of what similar properties would cost in Britain, location is also a critical factor on this side of the Channel. Unlike in Britain, it has not yet become generally fashionable to live in the countryside, so rural properties are not seen as particularly desirable. The French like being beside the sea and will always pay for a view, so coastal properties command a premium. If we are to find an interesting new home at a reasonable price, it looks as if we are going to have to move to the inner reaches of the marshlands.

Today, we have been exploring the villages and hamlets around Sourciéville and calling in at bars and shops to ask local people if they know of any houses for sale. While Mark is doing his best to find somewhere suitable and at a good price in the north of the Cotentin, we have been doing our own investigating further south. This will widen our choice of properties at an affordable price, and if we find somewhere by using local knowledge we may be able to pick up a real bargain.

If you are looking for a house up to a thousand miles from where you live in Britain and do not have a strong command of French, it makes obvious sense to use an agent based in the area where you wish to buy. As well as sending you details of available properties, your agent will take you on a viewing tour and negotiate the price when you have found what you are looking for. He or she will also see you through all the stages from the initial contract to completion, and help you arrange all the details of registering with the utility services. For this, your agent will naturally expect a fee, and in the reverse of the normal situation in Britain it is the buyer and not the seller who pays the agency for its services. The size of the fee will depend upon the price of the property. But we know that, although most French sellers will register with a specialist property agent, there are still many who prefer to put the business directly in the hands of their local notary. He is obliged to display details of the properties he has on his books, and can also be a valuable source of information about houses that will or may be coming on to the market. Every town will have at least one *notaire*, whose job is to officiate neutrally over all property transfers in the area and collect all monies due to the government. Apart from the fee for his services, both the buyer and seller of any property will be faced with a number of additional impositions thought up by the ever-imaginative minds of those whose job it is to raise funds for the running of the Republic.

Although I had thought that we had passed by if not through every commune in the Cotentin, it has been a revelation to travel deep into the interior and discover places we had not known existed. We have found hamlets and even whole villages that do not appear on the most detailed of maps, and some which appear not to have been visited by outsiders for generations. We have also found and looked at some properties that appear not to have been lived in for generations, if at all. The good news is that prices are markedly lower in this isolated and often brooding area of the peninsula; the bad news is that we have seen nothing which caused even a flicker of interest. But we have seen some remarkable buildings masquerading as homes, and I have added to my list of lean-to extensions that defy all the rules of physics and gravity by remaining fairly upright. As some men like to collect and list sightings of birds, trains or planes, I like to seek out and mentally register a number of features which seem particular to rural France. One day when I have the time and money, I intend to publish a guide to some of the most unusual plumbing and sanitary arrangements in rural bars, and that could be followed by a homage to the creators of the most spectacular lean-tos. The French for what we would call an outbuilding is *dépendance*, and some of the most rickety examples I have seen certainly live up to their name.

Apart from these rewarding sightings, we also met with some characters and situations which prove that I do not need to invent stories for my books about everyday life in our part of rural France. Dusk was falling, we had reached the end of our viewing list, and had found and looked at the outside of a property at the bottom of the longest and most poorly-maintained track I have encountered in all my years in Lower Normandy. As with the lean-to and toilet phenomena, some country people in our area seem to take a pride in creating records in the number of potholes they can achieve for each metre of the track leading to their homes.

While I was trying to close a broken gate outside what we thought was a derelict and therefore uninhabited cottage, Donella called a warning and I looked round to see an ancient Renault trundling down the track. It was heading straight for me, and had no driver. I immediately took cover behind the stone wall in front of the cottage, and heard and felt the car arrive. Climbing over the bonnet I looked inside, and saw an elderly man slumped in the passenger seat. Obviously revived by the collision, he stirred and grunted, then kicked open the door and staggered out. Ignoring us, he made a half-hearted attempt to open the gate, then gave up and simply threw himself over the wall. Crawling up the garden path, he disappeared inside his home. After closing the door of the battered Renault, I called a polite good evening to its owner and we set off to navigate the long and treacherous track back to civilisation.

*   *   *   *   *

We have solved the mystery of the driver-less car. I have also added to my list of interesting rural bars and their often unusual toilet facilities and arrangements.

A mile or so from where the track to the cottage joined the main road, we arrived at a small village. Alongside the church was a bar and grocery shop, run by a small, bird-like woman with a big and nervous-looking dog which seemed to be named after a chain of convenience stores. When we had settled down with a drink and had passed the time of day, I told Madame about our experience. After aiming a stream of invective at the dog when it tried to approach Milly, Madame explained that what we had seen was a weekly and quite normal occurrence. The man was a retired farmer, and liked to visit his old friends at the market at Sourciéville every Monday. After selling his farm, he had missed the camaraderie and hard bargaining, the general atmosphere, and most of all the prodigious drinking sessions when business was done.

To begin with, he would drive his car to and from the market, but after several expensive encounters with other drivers and the local policeman, the old farmer realised he would have to make other travel arrangements. He had many offers of a lift to and from the town, but could find nobody who would risk their suspension by venturing from the road and down the long and spectacularly unkempt track to his home. So, he had devised a system which would suit everyone. On the morning of a market day he would drive to the top of the track, turn his old car around in the road and leave it pointing downhill. He would then wait for the market bus to pick him up and take him to town. After the traditional session in the farmers' favourite bar, his friends would escort him to the bus for the return journey. At the top of the track, the driver and one or two passengers would help him to his car. If he were capable, he would then start the engine and negotiate the bumpy half-mile of track down to his home. If he were not feeling up to driving, he would simply unlock the handbrake and let gravity take its course. If he was beyond even that simple task, the bus driver would do the honours and send him on his way like a fallen Viking warrior laid out in his longboat and sailing towards the setting sun with nobody at the rudder. The track was fairly straight, said Madame, and generally the car made the journey to the house. The old farmer had even devised an ingenious arrangement of baling twine which could be lashed around the steering wheel to keep the car on course. If it did not complete its journey, the farmer would stay there till he sobered up enough to reach his home on foot. It was, she concluded, a very practical and logical solution to the problem. The man was helped by his friends at a time of need, and, most importantly, he had kept his independence.

Having agreed that it seemed a very satisfactory arrangement, I ordered another round, and when Donella asked for directions to the toilet, Madame explained that there were no facilities in the bar. In the traditional manner, men abused the wall of the alleyway alongside the shop; the occasional woman visitor in need of relief was always welcome to use Madame's private toilet. The shop and bar were rented from the people who lived above the premises, but Madame's home was just across the street. It was the small house with the green door, which my wife would naturally find unlocked.

While I waited for Donella, I asked the proprietor the origin of her dog's unusual name. She explained that, since a chain of grocery stores moved into the area some years ago her business had been on a downward spiral. At about the same time, the dog had turned up on her doorstep. She had tried to discourage it, but it would not go away. Like the rival store in the next village, the dog was costing her money and was a blight on her life, so she had naturally called it Proxi. It was a badly behaved dog, she added, so she was constantly required to chastise it. Although she could do nothing to halt the decline of her business or get rid of the dog or the nearby grocery franchise, she found it gave her a little satisfaction to have the opportunity and excuse to curse the very name of the company which had given her such unhappiness.

As the lady came to the end of her story and shook her fist in mock-anger at the dog, my wife returned. When Donella said she had closed the door safely and had enjoyed meeting her family, Madame said that she had no family and lived alone. Further enquiries revealed that my wife had gone through the wrong green door. She had, she said, found the toilet at the top of the stairs, then returned to have a brief chat with the family who were eating dinner in the front room. They had, she said, seemed friendly if a little bemused when my wife had explained she was just passing through, and had even wished her a safe onward journey.

As she waved us on our way, Madame said that my wife

should not be embarrassed by the mistake. It was, in a way, poetic justice that she had made a convenience of the family's home as they now did all their shopping at the rival grocery store in the next village.

*　　　*　　　*　　　*　　　*

The deadline draws ever closer, yet we have not found a new home or received any offers on La Puce. Our agent arrived with several potential buyers this week, but none seemed interested. There was either too much land or too little, or the property was located too close to the main road or too far from the nearest town. One couple said they had not realised there would be so much water at a water mill. Another fleeting visitor explained she was an artist and looking for an atmospheric and peaceful setting to inspire her, but was disappointed that the mill cottage had no view. She had hoped it would have been on a hilltop with a striking panorama, not buried in a valley and surrounded by trees that stole the light. I explained that because rivers tend to run downhill, water mills were generally built at a lower level than the surrounding landscape, but my attempt at sarcasm was obviously wasted.

I am now beginning to wonder if we will actually find a buyer, and that is worrying. At other times of financial crisis we have put La Puce on the market to stall our creditors, but have never before made a real effort to sell. Last year, my wife spent much of her time putting potential buyers off by pointing out severe and sometimes even imaginary defects in the fabric and structure of all the buildings at La Puce. Now we are in desperate straits and will probably have to sell, it is frustrating that nobody seems interested in an unusual property which is known to many thousands of people around the world. When we discussed the best way of attracting potential buyers, I suggested to Mark Berridge that it might be an idea to market

La Puce as the home of a fairly successful author and his wife. He said that he had already tried that approach but it had been unrewarding. The people who replied to his advertisements were either unimpressed by the possible cachet, or had read my books and were put off by all the things I had previously written about the condition of the property and the problems we had with poachers and weird neighbours.

Now that the situation is becoming really serious I am making a last attempt to raise a lot of money in a short time. Yesterday, I called Didier Bouvier and asked about expanding our language school and student placement scheme, but the news was bad. He said that most of the local people had told him they were giving up trying to learn such a complicated and illogical tongue. There had also been certain problems with the placement scheme that he would explain when we next met. He did offer me a case of his vitality tonic at wholesale price, but refused credit and would not tell me the recipe or if it really worked. Whatever is in the tonic, it is certainly effective, as Patrick the Post is fast becoming a living legend in the area. Not only has he registered with Jean-Claude's escort agency, but his moped has also been seen outside the houses of a number of young women while their husbands are out at work. As at least two of the ladies are not on his round, whatever else he has been delivering it has certainly not been letters.

*   *   *   *   *

There is the slimmest of chances that our money problems may be over, and La Puce saved.

Since I began investigating money-making schemes on the Internet, my electronic post-box has been overflowing. This morning there were more than a hundred business propositions, all offering to make me rich in a very short time. One message claimed that the sender had made more than ten thousand dollars in his first week of working for no more than an hour; all I had to do was use my credit card to send him a small sum and share in his secret and the proceeds. As any credit was removed from our cards by Mr Connarde last week, I was not tempted. Anyway, I think I already know the secret of my would-be partner's alleged success. Like all the other invitations to become rich quick, his e-business is nothing more than a modern version of a global chain letter. Thousands of people like him have obviously fallen for a similar invitation, and now they have to persuade thousands more to send them some money and join in the scheme. Most of the other proposals I received this morning probably came from his latest customers, rushing to sign me up before he does. Last year, I was persuaded to join a similar scheme which took the form of finding passengers for an imaginary aeroplane. After I had paid for my ticket I had to enrol further fellow travellers and pass their money on to my contact. With each success I would be moved towards the front of the plane, and eventually take the pilot's seat. When this happened, I would receive a thousand pounds. When I finally reached the cockpit and did not receive my reward I managed to contact the organiser, but he said that the plane had unfortunately crashed with no survivors.

But amongst all the chain-mail propositions, there was a story which is so implausible it might just be true. The message allegedly came from a Nigerian cabinet minister. He says that he has heard of me and what an honest person I am, and that I might like to help him, his country and its people in return for a significant cash reward. Colonel Objuku believes that a right-wing coup is imminent, and it is vital that the Ministry of Finance moves its cash reserves to a safe place during this period of crisis. To ensure that the money is untraceable and irretrievable by the rebels, he is contacting hundreds of totally trustworthy people like me to ask if they will look after a proportion of the funds. When and if the crisis is over, I will be asked to return the money to him. Whatever happens, I will be paid a handling fee of one hundred thousand Nigerian pounds. All that he needs for the transaction to go ahead are the details and number of our bank account and credit cards so that he can make an immediate transfer of several million pounds. I do not know the value of Nigerian pounds and may be clutching at straws, but have sent all our details. Unlikely as it may appear, if the letter is genuine our money problems will shortly be at an end. If it is a hoax it will make no difference to our situation, as our credit cards are no longer valid and the only sum in our account is in the form of a very large overdraft. It is also pleasant to picture Mr Connarde's face if he were to idly take a look at our account and see that all the zeros now had a positive number in front of them.

*   *   *   *   *

It has been a sad end to a bad month. Donella needs to be alone, so I have come to talk to my old friend Lucky at the Hobbit tree. Earlier today, we took Cato to the veterinary surgery at La Haye-du-Puits and have returned without her.

She had grown steadily weaker since the vet diagnosed her cancer, and Donella spent every moment of her last days with her. They lay together on the sofa in the mill cottage, with Donella cradling Cato in her arms and occasionally trying to tempt her with an eye-dropper filled with cream. All the while, my wife would caress our cat and remind her of the good times of the past. Donella is a very practical woman and much stronger than me in many ways, but she feels a tenderness and compassion towards animals that can make my heart ache.

After we had said our goodbyes and the vet had slipped the needle in to Cato's leg, she gave a soft sigh and then lay completely still. When I reached out my hand to give her a farewell pat, her eyes opened and focused on me. The old feral gleam flashed momentarily, and before I could react she struck out and drew her claws down the back of my hand. Then, as if she had used up her last spark of energy, her eyes clouded over and her head fell back on the table.

When the vet had cleaned and put a plaster over my scratch, he closed the surgery and took us over the road for a drink. There were customers in the waiting room, but none complained when they knew where he was going and why. For a half hour, we sat and told him about the adventures we had had with Cato, and he listened without embarrassment as we laughed and cried. Before he went back to work he said that the wound on my hand will probably not scar, but I hope it does. It will be good to carry a permanent and suitable reminder of such a special animal.

*   *   *   *   *

It has happened.

Donella was sitting with Milly at the grotto when Mark Berridge called to say that we have had an offer on La Puce. He had arrived with a couple while we were at La Haye-du-Puits, and they spent no more than an hour looking around before saying they would like to buy our home. They have returned to London and left their offer with us, and Mark believes, if we really intend selling, we should think seriously about accepting it. As we know, La Puce is not everybody's idea of the ideal property to have to manage by remote control, but he has been surprised by the lack of enthusiasm of the other potential buyers he has shown round. This couple seem genuine, but can withdraw their offer at any time without obligation until they sign the first stage of the contract. Sometimes when people return to Britain after seeing a property they are sure they want to buy, their enchantment fades. From a distance and away from the first burst of excitement and enthusiasm, they begin to have second thoughts. If we do want to go ahead, Mark recommends that we sign our side of the *compromis de vente* as soon as possible so he can post the contract to them. He does not want to put pressure on us, and will understand if we change our minds. But if we are sincere about selling La Puce, we must act soon.

As if I am listening to someone else speaking, I tell Mark that I will talk to Donella in the morning. Until now, I had never really believed that we would be selling La Puce, or that his call would come. I know that he needs an answer, but I must speak to my wife before giving it, and she has other things on her mind at this moment.

Part Three

It cannot rain but it pours.

Title of a pamphlet allegedly written by Jonathan Swift in 1727.

June

A perfect summer day, and to me La Puce has never seemed more beautiful.

Our hedgerows have been transformed by an explosion of snow-white elderflower and the water meadow is a field of gold. The land itself seems bursting with promise and vitality, and I wish I could paint well enough to capture this moment and keep it forever.

My wife and I spent most of the morning discussing the offer to buy La Puce, and what we should do about it. I spent the first hour trying to persuade her that we should take our time before signing the contract, as something might happen to give us a last-minute reprieve. We might hear from one of the dozens of minor publishing houses to whom I sent the manuscript of the new book. Or Mr Connarde might have a change of heart on calling in our overdraft. We might even come up with the right numbers to win the National Lottery. Having heard my arguments, my wife said that our neighbour's pigs might also start practising aerial manoeuvres above the water meadow. We both know what has to be done, and must get on with it. Hesitation could lose us the sale, and we will only feel worse about leaving our home if we draw out the agony.

We cannot be sure that the couple from London will not change their minds, but if they do go ahead there is still the small matter of us finding a new place to live. Whatever happens, we have to sell La Puce. There is no realistic choice, so we must sign the contract. For all the reasons which should be obvious even to me, we must bite the bullet and sign.

I know she is right, though I still find it hard to believe we are about to sign away our home of thirteen years. I have always been the sort of person who prefers not to think too much about problems before they become critical, and I had convinced myself that something would turn up and solve our financial nightmare. Now I can see that, one way or another, we are going to lose La Puce.

*   *   *   *   *

Life goes on, and I am in the caravan, dealing with a torrent of e-mail messages. Counting the contents of my electronic post-box, I see that the day has brought more than two hundred suggestions on how I can get rich quick or set out on a new career path. Amongst them is a two-week correspondence course in cosmetic surgery and the offer of a starring role in a porn film if I have the right dimensional qualifications. There is also a book for sale called *1001 Ways To Make Money From The Internet!*, and it seems as if everyone who has bought it has also got hold of my electronic address.

I can find no message from Colonel Objuku, so must assume that either the coup has been called off or he has changed his mind about asking us to look after several million pounds of Nigeria's cash reserves. I know that he has not transferred the money to our bank account, as I spoke to Mr Connarde earlier and there was no remission in his increasingly patronising and otherwise offensive manner.

154

When I told him that we had been made an offer for La Puce, he sounded quite disappointed and said I should not count my chickens before they are hatched. I said I was a little tired of hearing that expression lately, and that our buyers were paying a small fortune for the property. He replied that he had heard English people would pay crazy amounts for any old ruin in the French countryside, but had not realised some of them were that naïve. When I asked him if the good news meant that he would defer the date by which we had to pay back our overdraft, he said that he would give me an answer when he had seen the contract. And he would want to see it signed by our alleged customers and attested by our *notaire*. To lighten the tension between us, I told him the old joke about a verbal contract not being worth the paper it is written on, but he completely missed the point.

*   *   *   *   *

I have dealt with all my correspondence, including some worrying e-mails from the readers who I chose as hosts for Didier Bouvier's foreign placement scheme. Eight of them have sent a message to say that their guests have disappeared. In each case, the student arrived, stayed for a day, then packed up and left with no explanation after receiving a call from the organiser of the scheme. All the hosts say they have received no money from Didier, and one said that the family car went missing at the same time as his guest. A reader from Ealing says that he is very angry about an incident featuring my student, his daughter and a loofah in the bathroom, and another said that he does not believe that his fleeting guest was French. He said that he had spent some time working in Eastern Europe, and the language he heard his lodger using during his telephone conversation with a mystery caller sounded much more Albanian than Basque.

155

We are at the Château Epinguet, ready to sign the contract to sell La Puce. Fiona is up a ladder trimming the two tall palm trees guarding the entrance to her stately B & B enterprise, and the mountain of septic tanks in the driveway has been replaced by a huge pile of ancient radiators that Mark says he bought as a job lot from a demolition contractor in Essex. Like sound roofs, adequate heating arrangements are something that many British buyers overlook when buying in the Cotentin. The winters here can be long and cold, and Mark says he will be able to let his clients have the radiators at a good price. They are of an early manufacture, impressively massive and made of cast iron, and I agree with him that they will look more suitable in older buildings than the modern and bland designs. There has been a problem with the suspension of the small van in which he brought the giant radiators over from England, but with the amount of time he spends on pot-holed Norman tracks, Mark is used to a bumpy ride.

Sitting at the table under the disinterested gaze of George the boar, we have been going through the first-stage contract and at the same time catching up on the current state of the laws governing the exchange of property in France. It is a long time since we sold our first home in Normandy and bought La Puce, and it seems many of the rules of engagement have been amended. Predictably, it seems that rather than being simplified, the process has become even more complicated, and especially when concerning foreign buyers. Mark has also told us that there are some small complications with the proposed arrangements between the buyers and ourselves.

As he explains, when we have signed the contract he will post it immediately to London. After our customers have added their signatures and the date, they will return the document to Mark and he will physically put it in the hands of our local *notaire*. Mr Remuen will then take over and prepare everything for the *Acte Finale*. This is the official completion of the sale, which will take place in his office at a time and date convenient to all parties. Although there are two separate stages to the transaction, Mark reminds us, the initial contract is virtually as binding as the final document. Our customers will be agreeing to buy La Puce at the price stated and in the condition of the property on the day they take over. We will be agreeing to sell it to them at that price and on the agreed date, and there can be severe financial penalties if we withdraw. However, as long as the notary agrees, any number of reasonable (and sometimes completely unreasonable) suspensive clauses may be written into the contract to avoid penalties in the case of withdrawal. The most common get-out clause relates to the buyers not being able to secure a mortgage on the property, but our customers will not be seeking a loan. I ask if it is possible to insert a clause that we can withdraw from the sale if we win the Lottery, or otherwise find the money to pay off our overdraft before completion date; Mark thinks this would be a good idea, but says that Mr Remuen, though a helpful and understanding man, is not likely to agree to this proviso.

As to the most suitable date for the *Acte Finale*, Mark says that our buyers are anxious to complete in the near future. When I ask how near in the future, he says they have asked to move in to La Puce no later than two months from today. He realises that we have not yet found a new home, but advises that we agree lest they lose interest and look elsewhere. He also knows that we need to settle our debt with the bank by that date. My wife and I look at each other, then nod agreement.

As our agent indicates where we must make our signatures on the contract, he says the buyers wish to make another specific and rather unusual condition. They do not have a French bank account, and for some reason do not wish to pay for La Puce in euros. If we agree, they will arrive on the day of completion with a banker's draft made out to pounds sterling.

In all his years in helping people buy property in France, Mark says this is the first time he has heard of buyers making this condition. Perhaps they are worried about a sudden downturn in the exchange rate at the time of the sale, or perhaps they are just not comfortable dealing in a foreign currency. For whatever reason, our buyers are insistent. But, as we will know, a bank draft is as good as cash, and any change in the rate by the time the completion date arrives may equally well be to our advantage. The euro has been strong against the pound in recent times, but all the forecasts are that what goes up must come down. If that happens we would receive a considerable bonus. Most importantly, Mr Remuen has agreed to the arrangement. My wife and I exchange looks again, then Donella nods agreement. Finally and before we commit ourselves, says Mark, he hopes we realise there may be some capital gains to pay on the profit we will, at least on paper, be making by selling La Puce.

I laugh without humour, and say that this is the last thing we need to worry about. Although the sum we are receiving for La Puce is more than ten times what the property cost us, we shall actually be losing money on the deal. We bought the two completely ruined buildings thirteen years ago, and in real terms have spent much more on the property than the selling price. Apart from the cost of completely restoring the mill cottage and farmhouse, we have spent tens of thousands of pounds on the grounds over the years, to say nothing of the many thousands of hours of unpaid labour we have invested. I know that as my friends in the Jolly Boys Club say, there is a tax on everything you do in France and that will likely soon include farting, but I am sure that we will make no gains - capital or otherwise - on selling La Puce.

In spite of my confidence Mark looks concerned, then gives an almost gallic shrug and says it is none of his business but he thinks we will need to talk quite urgently to Mr Remuen about the situation. After a moment of silence broken only by the ticking of the long-case clock in the corner, he clears his throat and asks us if we are ready to sign.

I look into my wife's eyes for the third time in half an hour, then reach for my pen.

*   *   *   *   *

We have been on a sentimental journey and have stopped for a drink at our first local in Lower Normandy. On the way home and feeling low, we crossed the Route National at Brix and took the back roads to Valognes and on to the hamlet of Yvetot Bocage. It is the way we drove with Mark Berridge nearly fourteen years ago to see what would become our first home in France. We had a very limited budget and even less idea of what we were seeking, but Mark came up trumps when he showed us the Little Jewel. As it turned out, we were to sell *Petit Bijou* quite literally before the new paint on the living room walls had dried, and I have always felt that we did not really get to know the little cottage or give it the attention and affection it deserved. The characterful stone building with its sharply pitched roof is still in the same caring hands in which we left it, and looks somehow contented. As we sat outside and recalled the small adventures we had had there, I said it was strange to think how different our lives would have been had we stayed a little longer. If nothing else, we would probably not be deeply in debt and having to sell our home. Donella reminded me that I had persuaded her to sell the Jewel, but also that if we had not moved on we may never have found La Puce or met and made all our friends at Néhou. This might have been a blessing when thinking of what some of my friends are like, but we would also never have known all the animals we have raised and loved over the years. She would never have met our darling Cato, and I would not have found Lucky. My wife is not

159

a sentimental or superstitious woman, but I know she believes that fate rather than self-determination sometimes guides our destiny. As she says when we have a particularly serious falling-out, someone or something must have arranged for her to meet, marry and spend more than half her life with me. Obviously, no sane woman would have volunteered for such a sentence had it been a matter of self-determination rather than an unavoidable fate.

*　　　*　　　*　　　*　　　*

An hour has passed and we are still sitting at a table in the window of the *Café de Paris*.

Perhaps because our lives are about to change, I find it reassuring to be in the bar where we would come to relax after a long day of working on the Little Jewel. It was here that we sat with the key to our new home on the table between us and realised that we had made our dreams come true. It was in the *Café de Paris* that we would celebrate small triumphs or console ourselves after a setback. Now we are here to mark another milestone on our journey through our lives in France. Outside, I see that the same people are still going about their business in what is said to be the largest square in Normandy. The boys who would race their mopeds up and down the cobbled pathways all those years ago have married the girls they were trying to impress as they performed their tricks, but a new generation of acrobatic suitors have taken their place.

Inside the bar, things seem to have changed little. Although a little greyer in the hair and even more florid in the face, Freddo the patron is still on duty behind the bar and the customers are still betting on when the ever-lengthening ash on his cigarette will fall into the glass he is filling. His wife Collette is still waiting at table and showing genuine interest in and concern for her customers and their lives. Most reassuringly of all, Collette's aged mother is still wielding her broom and sharing a joke or few sharp words with those she thinks deserve them. In her time she has dealt with drunken German occupiers and marauding English hooligans, and I suddenly realise that I have never asked her who she found most difficult to control.

I signal for another bottle of Normandy champagne, and ask Collette if there is still room on my slate. She says that it is a very big slate, and leaves us to talk about the immediate future. I say to Donella that now we have signed the contract, I have accepted that we are to leave La Puce and I realise what lies ahead. Together with negotiating all the complexities of selling our home, we have to find a new one in less than two months. With no credit facilities at the bank, we shall probably have to move out of La Puce and in to our new home on the same day, with a lengthy session in the notary's office in between. And this will not be like any other move.

We shall have to clear out and transport all our furniture, furnishings and possessions from the two buildings at La Puce, and also everything that must be moved from the ten acres outside. This will include the contents of the outbuildings and my tool sheds, my stores of building materials, and perhaps even the caravan by the big pond. As I start to make a rough list on the back of a beer mat my wife says that I have forgotten to mention our animals and her special things. Apart from Milly, there are the chickens, Ermintrude the balletic goose and Hen the duck, and we must take at least a selection of our crayfish, frogs and goldfish. Then there is everything in her potting shed and greenhouse, and cuttings from her favourite plants. There are also dozens of young trees still in pots, and she thinks the new buyers will not object to her taking some of her favourite shrubs. There are several hundred planted around the grounds of La Puce, and she will want to take no more than a dozen.

Without thinking to engage my brain before opening my

mouth, I say that we have more important things to consider than a few cuttings, and it will be hard enough work shipping our chickens across the peninsula, without worrying about whether a dustbin of goldfish are suffering from travel or homesickness. It is almost a relief that we will not have the problem of capturing and caging Cato for the journey. Donella falls silent and I realise what I have said. I start to apologise, and for the first time since I have known her, my wife begins to cry in public. Reaching out towards her, I say that I will ring Mark now and tell him to tear up the contract. There must be some other way of paying our debts. I would rather rob a bank and go to jail than be responsible for taking her away from La Puce.

My wife smiles a resigned smile, wipes her eyes and says that, all things considered, that has been the best suggestion I have made for thirty-four years.

*   *   *   *   *

Six weeks and five days to go before the *Acte Finale* is to be signed. We are sitting outside Mr Remuen's office, waiting for our first meeting to discuss the sale. His diary has been completely full of appointments with other customers, but he has agreed to see us during his lunch break. That a Frenchman is prepared to delay or even miss his mid-day meal is not only a signal that he really is very busy, but also how the level of property exchange in rural France is escalating.

As we wait, I flick idly through a magazine of properties on sale in the area. All those which look promising are twice the price we have budgeted for, so it seems certain we shall have to move to a cheaper part of the peninsula. Yesterday, we took our tenth expedition into the Cotentin interior in as many days, but have yet to see a single house that could become a home.

162

The door to the office eventually opens and an elderly couple emerge, followed by Mr Remuen. He is as tall and spare as they are short and wide, and he leans down towards them as they shake hands and exchange farewells. The man is wearing a green bib-and-brace overall and brown wellington boots, and his face records at least sixty years of exposure to summer sun and all-year-round wind and rain. He has obviously kept his peaked cap on throughout the meeting, and now doffs it briefly as he turns to leave. The woman has obviously made an effort to dress up for the occasion, and despite the warmth of the day has chosen her church-going black coat, which is buttoned severely up to the neck. On her head she wears a smart bonnet that must have seen as many weddings and funerals as her husband's face has seen seasons of the year.

Mr Remuen is in his shirtsleeves, and boasting a silk tie that would give a chameleon a nervous breakdown. On his wrist is an elegant designer watch, and on his feet an equally smart and expensive pair of casual shoes. For me, these three people and their reason for meeting is an almost perfect example of the changing times in rural France. I know from their parting conversation and the slightly dazed expressions on the faces of the elderly couple that Mr Remuen is arranging the sale of their house to an English buyer. They will soon have more money in their savings account than the man has probably earned in half a lifetime of hard work, and I saw Mr Remuen's smart new car parked outside when we arrived. For the moment at least, everyone seems to be benefiting from the British invasion.

After seeing the couple off the premises and glancing at his watch, our notary hurries over to apologise and usher us towards his office. Inside, we take the two chairs facing his desk, and I notice they are still warm from contact with their previous occupants. As we settle down and talk about the weather, I have a sudden premonition that we will be spending a lot of time in this office over the coming months. I don't know why I am feeling so nervous, as we should by now be familiar with what lies ahead. This will be the second time we have bought and sold a property in France, and I receive hundreds of e-mails and letters a year from readers who have gone or are going through the process. On reflection and thinking about our past experiences and some of the horror stories I hear, perhaps my trepidation is well-founded.

Of all people, I should know that it is a general rule of buying or selling a house in France that something will go wrong. No matter how well the preparations are made, it is inevitable that something will occur to ensure a drama. Sometimes I think that it is written into the constitution that people wishing to buy or sell a property must be made to suffer. Sometimes, I think these problems arise or are manufactured simply because of the French love of theatre. It is another general rule that the French say that they loathe bureaucracy, but actually enjoy sowing and harvesting its fruits. I also believe they like creating so many regulations and laws just so they can bend, break or ignore them. Most if not all of the French people I have dealt with seem to relish creating problems so that they can take the credit for solving them. Or for refusing to do so. Anyone who has watched a farmer, shopkeeper, waiter or office worker gravely savouring the word *problème* will know exactly what I mean. While sitting in a chair like this one I have also observed that the average notary seems to work hard at finding a stumbling block that he will only dismantle when you are just about to fall over it.

In spite of my foreboding, I cannot see that we should have too many heart-stopping moments with Mr Remuen. It was he who oversaw our purchase of La Puce, and he knows in what condition it was in when we bought it and how much we must have spent on restoring it. He has driven past our home every day for the past thirteen years, and has seen how it has changed. I also know that Mr Remuen is a good and honest man, and that if there are any problems, he will do his best to make them go away. After, of course, he has built a suitably

164

high stumbling block. I know that this is not because he wants to put us through torment, but just the way the game is played here. Mr Remuen has the most expressive smile of any man I have met, and it can signal or mask any degree of good or bad news for his customers. I don't know if he plays poker, but I would not like to be at the same table with him when a big pot is at stake.

Our meeting begins, and Mr Remuen opens his bulky file on La Puce with the air of a surgeon making the first decisive incision. In the folder will be every scrap of paper relating to legal entanglements our home and its surrounding land have been subject to over the past century and beyond. There will be hand-drawn plans of the once constantly changing jigsaw of individual plots within the boundaries, and letters to and from their long-dead owners. The folder will also hold the deeds of the property and the contracts we signed in this office thirteen years ago. Although those years have sped by, I can still recall the exact moment when Mr Remuen put the key to La Puce in my hands and how I felt as I passed it to Donella. So much has happened since then, and our home has been the witness to so many moments of joy, frustration, occasional sadness and not infrequent farce.

While I have been travelling through time, our notary has been leafing through the papers in our file, and now looks up with the expression of a man who has good and bad news to impart and is not sure which to announce first. As I begin a countdown to my estimate of when he will first use the p-word, he congratulates us on our sale and for achieving such a good price on the property. Our buyers have signed and returned the contract, and he anticipates no real difficulties with the transfer. There may, of course, be some small *problèmes* to overcome. As I congratulate myself on the accuracy of my forecast, Mr Remuen says he has yet to receive the passport photographs and other proof that our customers are who they say they are. Also, their condition that they will only pay with a banker's draft is most unusual. Normally, he would insist that the money for the purchase be in a French bank account four days before the completion date. After giving the matter much thought, speaking to our agent and talking with several colleagues in the region, he is prepared to proceed if we are satisfied with the method of payment. I nod agreement, and Mr Remuen continues. We will be aware, of course, that because of the difference between the price we paid for La Puce and the price at which we are selling it, the question of capital gains tax will arise.

I have come prepared for this issue, and reach for the metaphorical ace up my sleeve while he lists all the allowances which can be set against our alleged profit on the sale. Firstly, there is the five percent discount from tax liability for every year we have owned La Puce. Had we stayed at our home for another seven years, he says with a wry smile, the bill would have been wiped clean. Because we bought at the end of one year and are selling in the middle of this, two of the years will not be admissible, but that still means a discount of sixty percent from any liability. Then there will be the adjustments for inflation over the years, and the interest we paid on the loan we took out to help pay for La Puce. He has been making his first rough calculations, and has arrived at the remaining sum on which we will owe capital gains tax. This, of course, is before any deductions for the improvements we have carried out on the premises. With another grade of smile, he says that he knows just how much work we have undertaken at La Puce. He passes me the piece of paper and I look at it, sigh theatrically with relief and hand him my envelope.

Inside is an invoice from the British builder who carried out most of the restoration of La Puce. Although we used local labour and did much of the unskilled work ourselves, the amount on the invoice and receipt in the envelope comfortably exceeds our theoretical profit on the sale.

My moment of smugness at having won this hand

evaporates as Mr Remuen puts his winning card on the table. After unfolding the receipt and examining it, he smiles sadly, shakes his head and returns it. Unfortunately, he says, the document is not valid. If it were from a French builder, all would be well. Even if it were from an English builder who had paid his taxes in France, it would have been valid. As it is and although it is clearly a genuine document, it is inadmissible. He knows from the evidence of his own eyes that we have transformed La Puce from a ruin over the years, and knows how much it must have cost us. But the law is the law, especially in France, so it looks as if we shall have to pay the substantial duty on the profit he knows we have not made.

*   *   *   *   *

As usual when big problems arrive, we have come to the pub. We are alone in the back room of the Flaming Curtains, and Coco is at the bar continuing work on degreasing the back axle of his Land Rover. He is a sensitive man, and can see that my wife and I will not appreciate company at this time.

I am still in shock from Mr Remuen's estimate of our capital gains bill, and can now see no way that we can go ahead with the sale of La Puce. As my wife points out, there is also no way we can withdraw from the sale. The cooling-off period after we signed the contract has expired, and we are committed. We have no choice. We know that we shall not be making a profit, and so does our *notaire*. But the Republic demands proof of all the money we spent in restoring La Puce, and have changed the rules about what constitutes that proof.

As Mr Remuen explained as he steered me gently to the door like a paramedic escorting a traumatised victim from the scene of an accident, the law invalidating British builders' invoices only came into force this year. It was obviously brought in to encourage foreign home owners to employ French builders, and incredibly even for France, the new law is retrospective in that it applies to the time before it was invented.

Now we are really in trouble. If our notary can find no way around the problem, we will owe the French government almost twenty thousand pounds in capital gains tax. If we have to pay the duty, there will be barely enough left to pay off our overdraft and buy a very modest home. And my new book will have to remain unpublished.

*   *   *   *   *

It looks as if we are to be given a reprieve, and it may be possible to leap nimbly over our giant stumbling block.

Mr Remuen called today to say there is a way to make our *problème* go away. He knows that we employed a number of local craftsmen on the restoration of La Puce, and that they and our British builder will have bought their materials in the area. If he pretends that he has not seen our invoice and we can produce the evidence of what we have spent on building materials in the past thirteen years, he will be able to estimate what we will have paid in fees to our real and imaginary French craftsmen. He realises that I will not be able to produce any invoices from the local people who did or did not work on La Puce, but that will not be a problem. The permitted formula in these situations of trebling the cost of the materials used should arrive at a total which will just about defray our tax liabilities. What he is proposing is quite legal, providing he ignores the document I showed him yesterday. I told him that I had already forgotten what was on that piece of paper, and that I shall dedicate my new book to him.

*   *   *   *   *

Our reprieve is on hold.

We spent an increasingly frantic hour in the loft of the mill cottage after Mr Remuen's call, but have found no more than a handful of receipts for the tons of building materials we bought over the years. Donella and I are not enthusiastic keepers of accounts, and anyway, I could have no idea that our British builder's invoice would one day prove useless. Virtually all the tens of thousands of pounds worth of receipts have long been discarded or turned into bedding for the family of mice who live in our loft.

But I think there is a way out of our problem. Nearly all the materials used on La Puce were bought from a family-run building supply company in the area, and they are sure to have a record of them. In France, householders are required to keep telephone bills for a year, water bills for two years, and TV licence receipts for three. Serious documents like electricity and gas bills must be held for five years, and bank cheque stubs and statements for a decade. The laws on keeping business records are even more draconian, so Mr Branluer must have details of every penny we have spent at his yard.

*   *   *   *   *

Another stumbling block has been erected, and this one has been built by a very skilled craftsman. During our time in Lower Normandy, we have met some exceptionally helpful people, but Mr Branluer does not feature on that list. He and his family have been happy enough to sell us many thousands of pounds of building materials, but I do not think they like us. From what I have seen, they do not like any of their customers and we are, after all, foreigners.

When I called to ask for copies of the receipts for all the

materials we had bought from him over the years, Mr Branluer laughed as if I were making a joke. When I explained our situation and said that Mr Remuen would accept a signed attestation from him of the approximate total, he said he was horrified that I should suggest a collusion to rob the government of its dues. In any case, what I asked was not possible as he had recently sold his business and was now acting merely as a consultant to the new owners. All his records were locked away for safe keeping in a vault at his bank, and his secretary had retired when the new firm took over. If he were to help me, he would have to ask her to come back from her daughter's home in the south and go through all the books. For her to examine every transaction over thirteen years and find our entries would take a long time, and he would have to pay her a special fee as well as all her expenses. He would also have to make a small charge for all the work and time it would take him. I thought about my options for a moment, then agreed. Before hanging up, I asked him to be sure that his secretary checked the true version of the two sets of business records that I knew he kept, but he pretended not to understand what I meant.

*   *   *   *   *

We are on the road again, and completely lost. Our search for a new home has led us deep into the heart of the Cotentinese *marais*, and we have seen no signs of civilisation for more than an hour. Neither have we had many clues as to where we have been and where we may be heading. Our journey has taken us on a winding route through vast stretches of the central marshlands, and signposts are as rare as other vehicles. In rural Normandy a lack of signposting is unusual, so it seems that in this particular area the authorities do not want travellers to know exactly where they are. Perhaps, my wife suggested, it is the people who live here who do not want to advertise their presence. If I am going to rob a bank to get us out of our financial problems, she said, this would be an ideal area in which to hole up.

To add to the problem, we are now becalmed in a most unseasonable mist, which appeared suddenly like a shimmering grey wall across the road ahead. Our headlights can do no more than dent the swirling wraiths, and I have left the car to see what lies beyond the wall. The blanket of mist has also insulated us from any distant sounds of water or wildlife, and I am accompanied only by the sound of my own breathing. Just as I am about to turn and grope my way back to the car, a giant figure looms above me. When my knees start working again and I see the figure is not moving, I investigate and see that it is a life-sized portrayal of the Crucifixion made in local stone. Roadside shrines are common in rural France, but this one is a monster.

Happily, I know that shrines are always sited near habitations. As I move closer and the fog lifts momentarily, I see that this shrine does not as usual mark a crossroads. The figure on the giant cross has his back turned to a single lane which leads from the highway. There is no other clue that we may find life at the end of it, but we must take every avenue in our search for a new home.

The fog has lifted, but we have still seen no evidence of civilisation. Curiously and although the sun has returned, it feels noticeably colder than when we left the highway. Microclimates in France are not uncommon, but this one is obviously exceptional. As I shiver and wind the window up, I see a car in the wing mirror, and Donella wrenches at the wheel as it races by. It is travelling at a tremendous pace and I cannot see the driver, but I tell my wife to hang on to its tail as it must be going somewhere that there is at least one house, whether or not it is for sale.

171

We have lost the car but found a village. After a mile of tyre-squealing pursuit, we rounded a sharp bend and the road ahead was clear. There were no houses or tracks leading off the route, and even the yawning ditches on either side of the road could not have swallowed a car whole, so where it went is a mystery. The name of the village is also a mystery, as we have yet to see a sign announcing its presence. Apart from this, the habitation looks much like any other small Norman commune. A handful of dilapidated houses are perched alongside the road on the outskirts, and we have seen an apparently uninhabited water mill which looks quite promising. Although it is very close to the verge, there should be little noise from passing traffic as we have not seen another car since the mystery vehicle disappeared. The mill cottage has become worn and dishevelled by time and the elements, but is in a basically sound condition by Norman standards for old and unoccupied buildings. There is a bonus in that it still retains what looks like the original wheel. This is most unusual, and adds to the air of promise. A large and currently dry field which would have been the reservoir lies directly behind the cottage, and alongside runs a pretty stream which disappears beneath the ancient stone bridge which spans the road. The property could never match La Puce, but with the application of some hard work and a little imagination I think it could be just what we are looking for. We can see no *A VENDRE* sign, but this may not matter if we can locate the owner and make him or her an attractive offer.

In spite of the drop in temperature my spirits are up, and I feel destiny might have led us to our new home in the Cotentin.

As we turn into the village square, I see other promising signs. In front of the church is a parking area occupied by a tractor, a mobile grocery van and an interesting old Citroën. By its marking and blacked-out windows it is obviously a former police vehicle, and of the type and vintage seen bucketing around the streets of Paris in period *films noir*. As we pull up, I see that the van is standing in front of an equally interesting *pissoir*. Compared with the rather basic facility at Néhou it is quite a sophisticated affair, and has a roof as well as walls. In spite of these embellishments it has no door, and so falls reassuringly short of appearing pretentious. I also note that it is very convenient to the bar and grocery store opposite. Adding to the general appeal of the village centre is the shop next door to the bar and *épicerie*, which appears to specialise in the restoration and sale of clocks. Well, at least one clock, judging by the window display. The square is deserted, but as we cross the street I sense someone is looking at me and turn towards the graveyard alongside the church. Before its owner ducks below the low wall, I get a glimpse of what seems to be a very odd face. I blink, look again, then call a greeting to put him at his ease before we walk on.

Inside, the empty bar is unremarkable except for two curiosities. It is the only bar I have visited in France which does not have the walls festooned with mirrors advertising brands of beer, soft drinks and cigarettes. The premises also contain a rare treasure in the shape of an original zinc covering to the bartop. Once this type of metal surface was a common feature, and in Paris *le zinc* became an affectionate slang expression for any favoured local. Nowadays, nearly all of those once-characterful haunts have been turned into trendy bistros, and the ultimate irony is that many of them have replaced their old metal bartop with a fashionable but very pale imitation of the original.

Apart from these two anomalies, what could become my new local looks much like any other rural bar. It has a tiled floor and a scattering of mismatching tables and chairs, and in one corner is a pin-table machine of the same approximate age as the former police van outside. Through an open door I can see into the private quarters, where an unwatched television is broadcasting the French equivalent of the *Big Brother* programme. Behind the bar is the usual array of liqueur and spirit bottles and packets of sweets and cigarettes, and strips of scratch-cards hang from the shelf. There is also a large bottle with a hand-made label depicting a human skull and a poison warning. The bottle contains what looks like farm-brewed *calva*, so the proprietor is hopefully a man or woman of taste and humour.

I ring the imp-faced hand-bell on the bartop, and as Donella goes off to investigate the grocery department, a man appears through the curtain-covered doorway connecting the two premises. He is an open-faced and pleasant-looking individual, despite a nose that has been even more spectacularly broken than Didier's new business partner at Sourciéville. I can also tell from the set of his shoulders and how he moves that he is probably a premier division shrugger. The patron gives me his hand and a cheery welcome and introduces himself as Bernard. As he pours my beer, I say that we are looking for a home in the area and notice that his hand jerks slightly and causes the rim of the glass to glance against the side of the pump. He puts the glass on the counter, wipes the spilled foam away, then says that there are certainly many empty properties in and around the village, though few are officially for sale. The population of this part of the *marais* is dwindling, and not many people seem to want to live here nowadays. I ask why this is, and he gives an exploratory non-committal shrug and says he cannot say. He is a comparative newcomer himself, and has only been running the bar and grocery store for a few weeks. He used to be an executive with a national chain of food retailers, but always wanted to be his own boss. He bought the business for a very good price, and did not realise why he had got such a bargain until he and his wife and children had moved in. When I ask him what the local people are like, he looks at the door before saying that, as in any small and isolated community, they can be insular and

174

sometimes even odd to the eyes of an outsider. If one keeps on the right side of them, however, they are not a danger. The word for danger is the same in both our languages, and seems a curious one to apply to the population of a village. As I begin to ask him if I have misunderstood its use in this context, he asks if I would like a drink on the house. I thank him, and ask if he knows who owns the old mill on the road into the village. Bernard gives his answer with a subtle negative twitch of a collar bone, then says some of the regulars will be in later and one of them is sure to know.

As we talk, I tell him about the car that overtook us and then vanished, and his hand trembles again as he lifts his glass to his mouth. After gulping a mouthful of beer, he says that he does not recognise my description of the car, so it could not have been a local driver. I pretend not to notice his agitation, then am distracted by a movement in the street outside. A face has appeared at the window, but is gone before I can register anything more than a fleeting impression. I ask Bernard who it was, but he says he saw nothing, then offers me another drink on the house.

A little later, and my wife appears through the curtained doorway. She is laden with a selection of small packages, all artfully tied with variously coloured ribbons. I ask if she has found a rich admirer and solved our money problems, and she explains that she has unfortunately only been shopping at the cold counter. The choice was so great and everything looked so tempting that she could not make up her mind what to buy. A compromise was reached at the suggestion of Bernard's wife, so she has bought a small amount from every dish. It will not be wasted, as what we cannot eat will be a treat for the animals. I explain quickly to Bernard that this is not an insult to the quality of his food, and that it is quite normal for my wife's pets to dine on *haute cuisine*. He smiles, performs a low-level shrug of the perplexed-but-indulgent variety, then says he has heard about the English and the way they treat their domestic animals. I turn down his suggestion of a bottle of fine wine to help the members of our extended family wash down their meal, and then begin to investigate the contents of the packages.

Opening each one like an impatient child on Christmas morning, I see there is another good reason that we should try to find a home in this vicinity. Laid out on the bar is a cornucopia of meat preserves and cold collations, all created from simple and inexpensive ingredients. In a Paris restaurant they would be served up in tiny portions on a ridiculously oversized five-sided plate and be valued at more than a farm labourer's wage for eight hours hard work. Bought from this shop they will have cost a few euros and taste much the better for it.

Before us are the parts of animals that many people would not want to even think about eating, now transformed by their creator into classic Norman dishes. There is tripe in the mode of Caen, pig pudding, tongue of cow and tail of ox, sweetbreads in jelly and a rabbit terrine so strong and obviously fresh that I half expect it to bound from the bar in a bid for escape. To follow, we have rice pudding and slices of apple tart and a pot of what looks like, if such a concentration were possible, quadruple clotted cream.

As Donella begins to re-wrap the packages, she says that the sign above the display cabinet said all the dishes were home-made, and asks if Bernard was the maker. He looks at her as if she had asked if he did the odd spot of brain surgery in his spare time, then says they were indeed all made at home, but not his. The food comes from the kitchen of the butcher in the next village, but the finer points of the French Trades Description Act have not as yet infected this part of Lower Normandy. I say they will taste none the worse for their journey, but our kitchen table is many miles away. I am not sure that I or the food will be able to last the long trek. Bernard takes my hint and says he will go and fetch some plates. He will also bring the bottle of wine he recommended for our pets so that we can see if it will prove suitable to accompany their supper. As he makes for his kitchen, I ask if he might also be able to provide a morsel of crusty bread, some *demi-sel* butter, perhaps a few gherkins, a dab of full-grain mustard and a sprinkling of garlic salt. He stops in mid-stride and I see his hand twitch again as he lifts it in an apologetic gesture. All the other things he can provide, he says, but he keeps no garlic salt in his kitchen or shop.

While we set about re-opening the paper parcels, Donella mentions that the shop is also out of garlic in its natural form, and when she asked Bernard's wife for a bulb, she said that they did not stock it as there was little demand from their customers. I agreed this was curious, but reminded her that the people of the *marais* were said to be a race apart from the rest of Normandy, and probably all of France.

*   *   *   *   *

We have had our first picnic on an original zinc bar, and it was a perfect setting for our feast. The empty plates have been cleared away, and I fear that our animals will miss out on their special supper.

The day is drawing to a close, and Donella is now concerned that we will not be able to find our way home. I say that we became hopelessly lost during daylight hours, so logic dictates that we will be put at no disadvantage by travelling in the dark. We also need to wait for the regulars to arrive so I can ask about the ownership of the old mill. Donella observes that it is getting very late, and the regulars seem to keep strange hours in this area. In our part of the Cotentin, the general rule and maxim is early to rise and early to the bar. I remind her that the people in this area like to follow their own ways, and that the locals have probably been in the fields and making the most of the good weather. It has not rained all day, although I see some dark clouds gathering above the spire of the church opposite. I think a summer storm may be on the way, and that would make our journey back to La Puce even more difficult. I propose that we wait to meet the regulars, and then I will treat her to a night in a nearby hotel. If it is good news about the mill, we will have something to celebrate. If not, we can continue our search in the morning. It is very unlikely that we would reach La Puce before dark even if we knew the way, so all she has to do is phone our neighbour and ask her to see the chickens to bed. My wife reminds me that there is unlikely to be a surfeit of hotels in this area, and that our cash reserves must last till we have completed the sale of La Puce. If we go on spending at this rate, we are going to be literally euro-less well before the date of the changeover. I remind her that our bank manager agreed to remove the embargo on our credit cards as soon as he saw the signed contract, and that Mr Remuen faxed him a copy yesterday. If she is worried about the expense of an hotel, I will ask Bernard about bed and breakfast establishments in the area. At worse, we can sleep in the car. We have done it before, and we will have Milly and her blanket to keep us warm. My wife looks as if she is going to protest, then says I deserve a break from our worries and goes off to ask Mrs Bernard if she may use the telephone. I realise and appreciate then that Donella has understood that I am reluctant to go home to La Puce and all the problems we are facing.

I am probably clutching at straws, but this is the first time since we started our search that I have seen a property and a place where we could possibly find contentment.

*   *   *   *   *

A regular customer has arrived, and he has a familiar and most unusual face.

The door opened to admit a flurry of wind, rain and a very strange figure. The man was exceptionally tall and his

178

angular body was enveloped in a sheet of plastic tied at the waist with baling twine. Above this bizarre parcel I registered an electrifying shock of red hair and a curiously asymmetrical face of the colour and texture of an overcooked pizza. I also noted he had the yellowest teeth I have seen in the mouth of a living person, and the lenses of his rain-spotted spectacles were as thick as the bottom of a cider bottle. It was the memorable face that I had glimpsed at the cemetery wall and through the window of the bar, and I could now see why he might wish to introduce it to strangers in measured stages.

The newcomer was introduced to me as Christian, and when I offered him a drink and asked his *métier* and if he had lived in the area for long, Bernard spoke for him. Christian, he said, was born in the area and does valuable work around the village. He is employed by the commune to keep the streets clean, tend the cemetery and maintain the *pissoir*. He does not say much, but takes his job seriously.

Shortly after he had settled in a seat near the window, I was to see that Christian takes his job very seriously indeed. After staring fixedly at the nearest table, he began to inch his hand towards an ashtray where a fly was taking its ease on the rim. The village's *agent de nettoyage* continued his stealthy approach, then pounced. His long fingers closed on their victim and he held his clenched fist aloft in triumph like a golfer who has just holed a tricky putt. Then he began to move his hand towards his mouth. As I watched in fascination, Bernard coughed sharply and Christian looked quickly towards him, hesitated, then dropped the dead fly in the ashtray like a dog reluctantly surrendering its bone.

Although I think this area may suit us well as a location in which to set up a new home, I am now beginning to realise why the heart of the *marais* has a reputation for being a strange place, and the properties here consequently so much of a bargain.

Summer storms are not uncommon in the Cotentin, but this one seems to have the energy and malignancy of a full-blown *tempête.*

Rain is streaming down the window of the bar and the squalling wind is doing its best to join us in the bar. The occasional flash of lightning illuminates the deserted square, and long rolls of thunder echo along the street. It is now highly unlikely that any more customers will arrive, and it seems we are in for an interesting night of camping in the car. Bernard says that there are no hotels in the area, and the idea of providing *chambres d'hôte* facilities for tourists has apparently not occurred to the people of this part of the marshlands. Our host is unable to offer us any proper accommodation, but says we are welcome to sleep on the sofa in the adjoining room. I can think of worse places to spend the night than a bar, but my wife says she will be uncomfortable with this arrangement.

As I say that she is likely to be more uncomfortable in the car, a sudden gust of wind throws the door open. I walk over to close it, then step back as a dark shape appears in the doorway. As if on cue, a searing flash of lightning is followed by an ear-splitting crack, and the figure steps through the door, looks round and bids us good evening in an educated, softly measured and modulated voice. Considering the appearance of the last person to enter the bar, I should be immune to further surprise, but our latest guest makes Christian look almost normal.

The man is tall and thin to the point of emaciation, and wears his silver hair pulled back in a tight pony-tail which reveals a sharp widow's peak. His features are gaunt and almost deathly-white, and there is a neatly trimmed moustache and goatee beard beneath his aquiline nose. While trying not to stare, I notice that his deep-set eyes are darkly rimmed and the eyeballs veined bloodily like the network of cracks on an old oil painting. His mouth is closed, so I am unable to see what condition his teeth are in, or how pointed and sharp the canines look. He is wearing what at first I take to be a billowing cape, then realise is a black overall draped across his shoulders which the buffeting wind is causing to flap like the wings of a great, menacing bird.

As he moves with an elegant glide into the room and approaches me, I smile nervously and cannot help but wonder if he is the reason that the bar has no mirrors on its walls, and the grocery shop next door is probably the only *épicerie* in all France which does not stock garlic.

*　　　　*　　　　*　　　　*　　　　*

The sun is shining and we are safely on our way home. As my wife said when we went to bed last night, my over-active imagination has been in overdrive. As I replied, a lively imagination is a valuable asset to any writer, even if I sometimes see things which are not really there.

Despite my misgivings of yesterday evening, it seems that Nulléplace is no more than a typical Norman village with the quite usual mix of diverse if sometimes unusual residents. The absence of signs on the road is because the authorities are replacing them with new ones in time for the tourist season. There was no garlic on sale at the *épicerie* because, as Bernard's wife had actually said to Donella, there had been a heavy demand and the shop had temporarily sold out. The bar had no mirrors on the wall simply because its owner does not like to advertise products he does not sell. I suspect that, because Bernard is a sensitive man, he also does not want to remind some of his customers what they look like. Most reassuring and interesting of all was the discovery that our red-eyed visitor is not one of the Legion of the Undead, and although aristocratic blood does run through his veins he has no interest in that which belongs to other people.

Henri Chartier is actually the owner of the clock repairing business next door to the bar. He is a Parisian by birth but has ancient roots in the area, most of which his ancestors seemed to own before the Revolution and *les sans culottes* removed the noble family's properties and heads at a stroke. Because the last surviving descendant of the Chartiers has to work for a living, he spends his week in the shop and travels to the capital at weekends to return the clocks he has restored. His face is so pale and his eyes so red because he sits in a darkened room looking through a magnifying glass during daylight hours. Due to his resulting sensitivity to strong light, he rarely leaves his home during the week until after nightfall, and then usually only to call in next door for a drink. When we had established his true identity and shared a drink, I confessed my earlier impressions and he was most amused. Although in these enlightened republican times he is not entitled to a title, he was flattered that I mistook him for nobility, though he says he would rather be known as the Count of Nulléplace than a close relative of the Prince of Darkness. When he learned that we were faced with a night in the car, he insisted that we take advantage of his spare room, and promised he would not look in on us as we slept.

I now have another good reason for searching for a new home in this area, as Henri is a cultured and charming man. He is also enormously well-read, highly educated and a deep thinker and philosopher in the best traditions of France. The walls of the room behind his shop are lined with books on every subject from architecture and anthropology to zoology and Zen Buddhism, and we sat long into the night talking of the ways of the world and the conceits and curiosities of humanity. Although I already have a number of French friends with whom I can discuss such metaphysical concerns, Coco Lecoq and the Jolly Boys Club will be many a mile away if we move to the *marais*. It is good to know that, while Nulléplace could never replace Néhou, there is at least one other village where we may be able to find some of the things we will lose by leaving La Puce.

Unfortunately, we will not be able to make an offer on the abandoned water mill, as Henri knows the owner and that he dislikes Britain and the British even more than other would-be newcomers to the area. However, Henri knows of another place which he thinks we may find even more suitable. It is a small but impressive *manoir* once owned by his forebears, sits at the bottom of a narrow dead-end lane, and looks out across around twenty thousand hectares of the central Cotentin marshlands. The location, he feels, would suit an *auteur* like me perfectly. Unlike in his ancestors' days, all the enchanting and fertile terrain it commands does not go with the house, but there are more than enough acres for sale with the property to keep even my wife happy. Henri does not know the price of the *petit manoir*, but thinks it will be a fraction of its perceived value elsewhere in the Cotentin. The property is not officially for sale, but he knows the owners wish to move to a smaller house in the nearest town, which is seven miles away. If we are prepared to put up with the isolation, the sometimes dramatic weather and, of course, having the Count of Nulléplace as a near-neighbour, it might suit us very well. In fact, we might even get to like being the lord and lady of this bijou *manoir*.

As we reach the oversized shrine that guards the lane leading to what could be our new village, I say to my wife that life has a funny way of leading us on to new adventures and experiences. Although I am sad at the thought of leaving La Puce and we have been too busy to really consider what is happening to us, there may now be something to look forward to. As well as having a very fertile imagination, any writer needs constant stimulation and new experiences and situations to invigorate its powers.

Donella agrees, though says we of all people should know not to count our chickens before they are hatched. If the manor house has not been sold yet and is within our budget, it may be what we are looking for. If it is big enough, we will be able to offer bed and breakfast accommodation to help keep us from falling in to debt again. But that, of course, depends upon the little matters of our avoiding the swingeing capital gains tax on the sale of La Puce, and the sale actually going through without any further and terminal stumbling blocks.

As we turn on to the main road, I tell Donella that I have a feeling that our minor tragedy may be turned into a triumph, and point out the spray of unfamiliar flowers someone has placed at the foot of the outsize shrine. When I ask her if she knows what they are, my wife smiles and says that perhaps my imagination is not, after all, that vivid. The surprisingly delicate and sophisticated blooms, she believes, are those of the *allium sativum liliaceae*, or common-or-garden garlic bulb.

When sorrows come, they come not single spies, but in battalions...

William Shakespeare, *Hamlet.*

July

Smoke rises lazily and hangs stubbornly in the breathless air. Like us, it is reluctant to leave La Puce. We have begun the great clear-out of all the things we will not be taking with us when we leave our home of thirteen years, and I have been making a bonfire of some of my vanities.

I am in the water meadow watching the flames devour dozens of boxes containing old manuscripts that will now never appear in book form or on any stage or screen. Although I like to think I am not overly sentimental, it is hard to see so many of my rejected literary efforts go up in smoke. The burning boxes represent not only my contribution to our agreement to travel as lightly as possible when we move, but also my determination to start afresh and jettison all unnecessary encumbrances from the past. At breakfast this morning my wife and I made a pact, and my smoke signals are also making a sharp point about keeping our sides of the bargain no matter how great the apparent sacrifice. In fact, I have kept copies of most of the burning scripts but wanted to make a dramatic gesture.

Yesterday, I found Donella working on her vegetable patch and was thoughtless enough to say she was wasting her time as we would be long gone from La Puce before her courgettes evolved into respectably-sized marrows. After spending some time quietly in her potting shed, she came out and started work again after saying that she had a duty to leave the patch in the best condition for the buyers and would anyway be taking any vegetables that could be transplanted at our new home. I said that even accepting her superior knowledge of horticulture, I did not think it feasible that a battalion of half-formed carrots could be taken out of the ground at La Puce, moved through time and space across the peninsula and then re-planted in the garden that we have not yet found.

I also said that we would not have room for a single embryo cabbage or cucumber on the removal van that I had not yet booked for the journey. If it would make her feel better, I would buy her a skipful of weary and cut-price vegetables as soon as we got to our new home and she could pretend that she had grown them herself.

After she had retired to the potting shed again and I had thought about what I had said and apologised and persuaded her to forgive me, we came to our arrangement. We would each draw up a list of items we thought we should be prepared to give or throw away, sell, leave behind or burn. Then we would compare notes and tick off those items on which we were in full agreement. In the case of disagreement, we would make a trade-off.

As I suspected, there was much disagreement. Most of the things I considered of little or no use in the future, Donella believed to be essential. Nearly every item on her list seemed to be one of my cherished possessions. Eventually we settled on a compromise, and every item of mine I agree to dispose of will be matched by one of hers. We have also established a neutral zone which covers items on which we will make a decision at the last moment. These include all my bottles of nettle champagne, the pick of Donella's vegetable bed, and the much-loved but now irretrievably defunct cement mixer that she has converted into a giant and very distinctive plant pot.

*   *   *   *   *

A bitter-sweet interval earlier today when we packed the first box of keepsakes.

Sitting in the loft, we sifted through the hundreds of photographs which record our time at La Puce and the gradual blossoming of the buildings and land. In the way of these occasions, even the reminders of hard and unhappy times were remembered fondly. Amongst the *tableaux vivants*, Donella struggles uphill from the stream with a bucket of water to make tea and mortar, her face reflecting her pleasure at recreating an ancient journey on what has just become her own land. My mother stands between our late mayor and his wife Solange, and Jean Chevalier poses as stiffly and proudly as if he were with the president of the Republic. I am caught in mid-swing as the sledgehammer makes its first descent upon the remnants of the cattle byre that is to become our bedroom. Our daughter stands with arms outstretched in possessive joy at the entrance to the water meadow, and our son clings wanly to the top of a rickety ladder after a night out with the Fox of Cotentin. Past and present members of the Jolly Boys Club rest from their voluntary labours alongside the tons of sand they have been shovelling into the gaping pit at the ruined end of the mill cottage, and René Ribet peers owlishly into the lens after falling off the roof during the topping-out ceremony at the farmhouse. Then, there are all the animals we have found, reared and loved across the years, and some that have been uninvited but eventually welcome guests. Big Albie the goose advancing on me with arched neck, flapping wings and murderous intent; the khaki campbell ducks forming a circle on the big pond as they come under attack from Psycho and his hordes of murderous goldfish; Reggie and Ronnie the Cray

187

twins in a drunken brawl following a feast of carrots marinated in best Burgundian wine; the Last Living Grouse in all Cotentin which appeared fleetingly on our land the day we bought La Puce; a blurred yet dazzling image of a kingfisher on his regular fishing trip to the big pond. And, of course, Lucky and Cato in all their moods and manners. With the photographs we found the old sweet tin containing the collars and identity discs of the dog and cat who strayed into our lives and hearts. My wife put the tin in the packing box as if it were made of the finest crystal. Our two old friends will not be coming on our final journey from La Puce, but their memories will stay with us forever.

*   *   *   *   *

Less than a month before we must leave La Puce, still so much to do, and still nowhere to live after the sale. The thirteenth day of August falls on a Friday this year, and I don't know if Mr Remuen chose the date at random or was displaying an unsuspected penchant for black humour. I shall have to ask my colleagues in the JBC if the date has the same gloomy significance in France. As the official name for fear of Friday the Thirteenth is the grimly impressive paraskevidekatriaphobia, I am sure that Patrick the Post and Michel le Scabeuse will want to add it to their vocabulary of ailments from which they allegedly suffer.

Tomorrow we are going to look at the *manoir* in the marshlands, but before that I have two important meetings. Later today we are seeing Mr Remuen to find out if the building material invoices will defray any capital gains demand, but before that I have to tell my friends in the Jolly Boys Club of Néhou about our move. It will obviously be a shock for them to discover that they are losing their only official overseas member, and they will naturally be worried that their club will

188

lose status with the departure of someone who is known to be a reasonably celebrated author in England. To be honest, some members will also regret the loss of the person who buys so many rounds of drinks when it is not his official turn.

*   *   *   *   *

As I should have known after living in this small community for so long, my shock announcement came as no surprise to a single member of the Jolly Boys Club. In fact, some of my colleagues seem to know even more about what has been happening in our lives than I do.

When I arrived at what is usually a poorly-attended weekday meeting, I found it difficult to park outside the Bar Ghislaine. Inside it was standing-room only, though I noted that a path was immediately cleared to the bar as I came through the door. It appeared that every past, present and still-surviving member had made the effort to turn up and mark the occasion and listen to me tell them what they already knew. Noticeable by their absences, however, were our rogue trader and the postman who now styles himself as the Stud of St. Jacques. The official excuses were that both were away on business, but Didier Bouvier has been avoiding me since the problems with our student placement scheme arose, while Patrick is doubtless doing his business with one of the members of what he calls his female fan club.

After I made my carefully prepared speech about our need to move on to a new home and area in my constant search for new people and places and situations to write about, there was a polite round of applause followed by a predictable rush for the bar as I invited all my friends and fellow-members to toast my health. While Madame Ghislaine struggled to cope with the demand, I was invited to join my special friends at the

189

table reserved for committee members.

Our president then conducted a simple but moving ceremony by saying how sorry he and the other members were to hear that we were leaving the area. Unlike the rest of the membership, the committee knew I had money problems and would otherwise never have considered leaving La Puce and all my friends. They also understood that I had invented my story about the reason for our departure as most of the rank-and-file members are convinced that by being English, keeping farm animals as pets and spending such a fortune on attempting to make a proper home out of an old water mill, my wife and I must be eccentric millionaires. The committee had realised just how serious my financial problems were when it heard that my wife and I were looking for a new home in the depths of the *marais*.

Young Pierrot then presented me with a framed photograph, taken at last summer's village *fête*. It showed Donella and I sitting at a table, with all our closest friends gathered around and raising their glasses to the camera. As our chairman said, if I were to hang it on the wall in our new house it would remind us of the good times and good friends we had made in our time at Néhou and the Mill of the Flea. While I cleared my throat, wiped my face and sniffed and complained of a summer cold, our president and official philosopher Jacques Délabré gave me a rolled sheet of thin cardboard torn from a beer pack and tied with a red ribbon. On the reverse side was a certificate made out in his best hand and confirming me as a lifelong member of the Jolly Boys Club of Néhou. In an attempt to distract my friends from my moist-eyed condition, I said he had forgotten I was only an overseas member and would have to buy another carton of beer and re-do the job. He smiled and patted me on the shoulder and said the committee had decided that, wherever the accident of fate had caused me to be born, as far as they were concerned I had proved myself to be a true member of their community and always would be, wherever in the world I travelled.

*   *   *   *   *

It is proving to be a rather emotional day, and I am sure there will be more to follow during the next month. According to one of our club members, though, all my preparations for leaving La Puce have been a waste of time.

When I had made the first of what is sure to be a series of long farewells and left the Bar Ghislaine, I was followed by our alleged prophet Luc Voiron. For the first time since I have known him, he is actually predicting an event before rather than after it has happened. Taking me by the arm as I was using the *pissoir*, he said that he had something very important to tell me. The previous evening he had experienced a startlingly vivid vision, and it concerned me and my future. Whatever I might think now, he said, I would not be leaving La Puce next month. In fact, I would never leave La Puce while I was alive. When I asked him what form the vision took and exactly what happened in it, he refused to say more and wandered back into the bar. He had obviously been taking full advantage of the free bar I had arranged, but seemed to be genuine in his concern and conviction. If he has at last made an accurate prediction, something is going to happen to keep us at La Puce. If the part about my dying there is accurate, I hope it will not happen until a very distant time in the usually unforeseeable future.

*   *   *   *   *

We are outside the office of our local *notaire* again, and are becoming such regular visitors that I am now on first-name terms with his receptionist.

After escorting another couple of dazed Norman house vendors from the premises, Mr Remuen ushers us in and we repeat our ritual of sitting on the still-warm seats and talking about nothing as he opens our case file. After studying the contents for a moment, he shakes his head, executes yet another of his sadly reflective smiles, and passes three sheets of paper across the desk. The first is a letter from our one-time building materials supplier. In it, Mr Branluer says that he and his former secretary have spent virtually every moment of the last week working together on his business records for the past thirteen years. They have been hard at it during both day and night sifting through the tens of thousands of business transactions noted in his ledgers, and he takes great relief and pleasure in enclosing an attestation to the sum total of the value of the materials purchased in my name from his business in the specified time period. He also takes pleasure in enclosing for my attention an invoice to cover the time spent on the project, and his former assistant's travelling, hotel and subsistence expenses.

I look briefly at the sheaf of receipts and see Mr Branluer's long-rumoured close friend as well as secretary has expensive eating habits and what must obviously be a very big car. I also note that in spite of her being a small woman, she booked a room with a double bed for her stay at the best hotel in Bricquebec. I then turn to what I at first think is the attestation by the large total at the foot of the sheet, but quickly realise it is only Mr Branluer's invoice. Moving on to the next sheet I scan it, blink, then read it again. At whatever distance and from whatever angle I view the attestation, the sum at the bottom remains the same. According to Mr Branluer, in thirteen years of buying tons of timber, shingle, sand and cement, countless packets of nails and screws, miles of copper and plastic piping and electrical wiring, dozens of doors and windows and their frames, hundreds of tools and other small items, to say nothing of veritable oceans of paint and woodstain, he vows that our total spending at his premises amounts to less than three hundred euros.

I sit and stare numbly at the sheet for a long moment, then look up at Mr Remuen. He gives a shrug which somehow conveys a mixture of sympathy, resignation and embarrassment, then adds another version of his sad smile. He says that he understands how much more I must have really spent at Mr Branluer's yard at Trichéville over the years. Clearly, Mr Branluer does not keep very accurate records, or not all of his transactions find their way into his business accounts. Although he cannot advise it officially, I should perhaps think more than twice about settling the invoice for my merchant's alleged work with his secretary. If there were any repercussions, I might even tell him I had been thinking about putting in a call to the income tax department for this area, and also perhaps to Madame Branluer to ask if her husband had been spending any time away from home of late. Although this tactic might well annul the invoice, it would do nothing to help my situation with the capital gains tax. However much of a hold I may have over him, Mr Branluer can hardly discover receipts that do not exist in his official records.

After allowing us to absorb the full impact of the blow for a full minute, our *notaire* purses his lips then adopts the air of a magician about to pull a rabbit from his hat and says that, although the continuing lack of building receipts constitutes a serious *problème*, there may be a way to solve it. Too weak to speak, I look imploringly at him and he explains. In cases like these, he says, there is what one might call a final court of appeal. When, for one reason or another, there are no receipts and invoices for work which has obviously been carried out, the owner may call in the services of an approved estimator. This specialist surveyor can be employed to visit the property, use his skills and training to assess all the materials used in any renovated part of the building, then calculate how much had been spent on them. He can also estimate the length of time each job would have taken, and allow an additional sum for labour charges. Mr Remuen estimates that the estimator's bill for his services is likely to exceed a thousand euros, but that amount will also be deductible from the alleged profit on the sale. With my permission, our notary will contact a highly recommended and approved estimator he has worked with in past and similar cases.

Even though I am wondering why Mr Remuen did not simply tell us about this avenue of escape in the first place, the rollercoaster that my emotions have been on throughout the day takes a sudden upturn, and I get up to make a celebratory jog around the deck. While at it, I will also leap nimbly over any other phantom stumbling blocks which may be lurking in my path. At last it seems we will be able to clear the capital gains tax hurdle with ease. Before I set off on my victory lap, Mr Remuen smiles his wryest of smiles, and says there is another quite significant *problème* which has arisen since we last met.

I slump back into my seat and wait for details of the next barrier on the path to our sale of La Puce. Steepling his fingers, Mr Remuen says that he had a call from Mark Berridge this morning, and is much concerned about a change of plan by our buyers. Rather than arriving with a certified banker's draft on the day of the sale, they now intend bringing a building society cheque. While our *notaire* knows that a British bank draft is unlikely to bounce, he is not familiar with cheques from what we call building societies, or how well they are underwritten. I do a passable imitation of a very bemused goldfish, then say that, at worse and if the cheque were to bounce, the sale would surely be declared null and void. Mr Remuen purses his lips again, then shakes his head and says I am mistaken. Once the *Acte Finale* has been signed in his presence, the transaction will have taken place and La Puce will belong to our buyers. If their cheque should not be honoured, I will have in effect and in law sold them our home for a piece of paper, regardless of its worth. The deposit they have already paid would be taken up with the fees due to Mark, Mr Remuen and France. Ironically, says our *notaire*, I will have given away La Puce for less than nothing, as I would still owe all our side of the fees and charges on the transfer, the cost of the estimator's services... and, of course, any residual capital gains taxes due on the profit we would not be making on the sale of La Puce.

*   *   *   *   *

It has indeed proved to be an emotional day. The light at the end of the tunnel has been switched on again, but it is on the blink.

After calling Mark Berridge, I spoke at length to the manager of our buyers' building society. When I asked if there was any possibility that her clients' cheque might bounce, she said that she could obviously not discuss their financial affairs and standing with the society over the telephone, and especially not with a complete stranger. When I explained the situation more fully and forcibly, she agreed to look at the records and see if any provisions had been made for the transfer. On her return she said quite sniffily that, as far as she could see, we had nothing to worry about. Our buyers had already made arrangements for the building society to issue a special cheque, drawn on their account. I would not be receiving a personal cheque from the buyers, but from the building society itself. Unless her company carelessly frittered away several billions of assets between the time I accepted the cheque and it was honoured, there would be no problem. As I thanked her and prepared to hang up, she did a fair impression of our *notaire* and said there could be a problem for us if the cheque were lost or stolen after the hand-over. Providing whoever stole or found it was able to cash or put it in their account, of course. She had never heard of that happening in England, but as we were talking about a foreign country...

I thanked her for her reassurances, made some enquiries

of our banks in Normandy and Hampshire, then went to warn my wife not to pack her sewing kit. If all goes to plan, we will get our hands on the cheque late on a Friday afternoon. Although our local bank will still be open, it has no facility to accept a building society cheque. If Mr Connarde were to make a special arrangement to do so, there would be a substantial charge and the bank's rate of exchange from pounds to euros would be punitive. Our best plan now seems to deposit the cheque in our English account, then have enough of the money transferred electronically back to France so that we can pay off our debts to the bank and buy our new home. The residue in England will pay for the publication of my new book. The real problem is that we cannot risk posting the cheque to England, so will have to physically take it back to where it came from in the first place. This means that, as well as moving out of La Puce and into our new home on the same day, we shall have to cross the Channel on that weekend and wait for the banks to open on Monday morning. The current owners of the house we have as yet to find will have to agree to wait for their money until it has crossed the Channel for the third time, and we will have to baby-sit a flimsy piece of paper worth more than a hundred thousand pounds for a whole weekend.

After discussing the best security options with my wife, I propose that we toss a coin to decide whether the secret pocket and the cheque it will contain should be stitched for safe keeping into my underpants or her brassiere. Donella refuses to gamble, and says that as a perfectly innocent man or woman at our bank counter in Hampshire will have to handle the cheque, she insists that in the interests of safety and hygiene she should be the bearer.

*   *   *   *   *

Now it seems we have cleared all the major obstacles to the sale of our home, we must turn our attention very urgently to the finding of a new one. I must also make arrangements for the moving of all our goods, chattels and livestock. We are to visit the *petit manoir* on the marshes tomorrow afternoon, and knowing what I know, I think it may prove easier to find a house for us to live in than an easy and economical way of moving the things that will go in and around it.

Though a stressful business, the average house removal in Britain consists of no more than choosing and booking a suitable company, then overseeing their work on the big day. In our part of rural Normandy and in our particular situation, the operation is going to be a little more complex. A standard-sized removal pantechnicon would completely block off the main road passing the farmhouse for hours on moving day, and to avoid chaos and possible carnage, I would have to go through the authorities and pay them to organise a suitable diversion, lots of official warning signs and at least two policemen to share arm-waving duties. Much more complicated will be the access to and loading of the contents of the mill cottage, the various outbuildings, and all materials and livestock from the fields. The cottage lies at the bottom of a narrow and winding track that was more than roomy enough for the biggest 18th-century grain cart, but will be far too narrow for the most modest removal van. The hump-backed stone bridge and tunnel of interlaced and overhanging trees that shroud the track will also be a problem for any large or high vehicle. I suspect I would also have difficulty in persuading the average removal company that four chickens, a duck, a large goose that thinks it is a duck, ten breeding pairs of frogs and other amphibians, at least a dozen dustbins full of assorted cray and goldfish and aquatic plants, together with several hundredweight of small trees, shrubs and immature vegetables are standard items for carriage. And that is to say nothing of an embedded caravan, two chicken coops and a former cement mixer now masquerading as a floral display. Even if I could find a professional company willing to take on the job, they would obviously charge a small fortune. But as I have learned during my time in Lower Normandy, there is always a way to achieve your objective at the right price if you go about it in the proper manner. I shall just have to organise the project myself, call in some favours and use my special contacts. A bottle of my best home-brew *calva* and a few euros slipped to a friendly off-duty motorcycle policeman should ensure his apparently official attendance to manage the traffic. I can ask René Ribet to acquire a handful of suitable road-under-repair, diversion and even unexploded bomb signs to add to the general air of official business taking place. I also have many friends with small lorries, large vans, versatile tractors and even earth-moving machines. With a few phone calls and the promise of free drinks and food after the event I should easily be able to summon a flotilla of vehicles and their drivers. I shall not tell Donella about my plans yet, as I know she will accuse me of trying to do things on the cheap and thus virtually guaranteeing a mammoth cock-up. But I believe that staging a carefully co-ordinated and supervised removal party will not only be efficient and cost-effective, but could also make for an interesting and enjoyable experience. The only major problem that I can foresee is the sale of La Puce falling through just as we complete the evacuation, and my friends having to move everything back again.

*   *   *   *   *

We are on our way to view the *petit manoir* near Nulléplace, and in spite of all her concerns I think my wife is quite looking forward to seeing what could become our new home.

On route to the marshlands, we will be stopping off so that I can do my duty at today's Grand Festival of the Carrot, and while Donella is ironing my costume I am attending to the morning post. She still has a vengeful glint in her eye as the effects of Didier Bouvier's vitality potion on our mailman seem to be escalating, and this morning he completely overstepped the mark. He arrived as my wife was bending over to earmark the vegetables we will be taking with us, and made some very lewd comments about the shape of her bottom and the small size of her marrows. Although she did not mind the remark about her bottom, I know Donella was outraged by the comments on her vegetables. When Patrick offered to show her something which would really keep her hands full, my wife asked him to wait till she fetched a magnifying glass, then returned with her miniature pruning shears and offered to undertake a size-enhancing transplant operation using her smallest and most misshapen courgette.

Now Patrick has buzzed off on his moped and in a huff, and I am sitting by the grotto reading my overseas copy of the *Daily Telegraph*. In the first of two otherwise unrelated articles that could explain the growing exodus from Britain to France, I read that England now sustains three hundred and eighty three people to the square kilometre. This is double the ratio to be found in Germany, and four times that of France. The article goes on to say that more than half the Britons questioned in a recent survey said that given the chance, they would prefer to live elsewhere, and the most popular destination was France.

On the facing page is an article claiming that people who live in rural areas of Britain are more than five times as likely to smile as those who live in cities or towns. The statistical evidence was garnered by researchers who stood on corners, smiling invitingly at passers-by and noting down their responses. Given what life seems to be like on some of the streets in the major urban centres of Great Britain, I hope the researchers were on danger money.

Putting the paper aside and opening my correspondence, I read a sad story from two old friends. They are great francophiles, and until two years ago holidayed regularly in

France. Both had well-paid and interesting jobs and a lovely home in the Kent countryside. The house was at the end of a secluded lane, with a church opposite and a pub renowned for its food and drink only a brisk walk away. But as retirement approached, the couple decided that they should follow their hearts, sell up and move to France. They were concerned that they would become bored in a comfortable and safe country home, and that life would pass them by. Before it was too late, they should embark on one last adventure.

Having sold their house for what seemed an almost obscene sum, they decided to rent accommodation in the south of France so that they would be able to take their time looking for the perfect location and property. For a year they ranged France fruitlessly during the day, and spent most evenings sitting in a hotel room with only each other and a wind-up radio for company.

After realising what they had left behind and how happy they had actually been with their old life, they decided to accept that they had made a mistake and go home. They even considered buying their old home back if the new owner could be persuaded to sell it to them. When they called a friend in the village to sound out the situation, he said their house had been demolished and three were sprouting in its place. He also told them that properties in the area had almost doubled in price since they had left. Now, they say, they are resigned to living for the rest of their lives in France but do not think it will be a happy time.

I shall write back and say how sorry I am to hear their news. It is a minor tragedy when people make decisions for the best of reasons but find things do not work out as they had thought and hoped. Curiously, I think that the only consolation they may find in time is that the home they loved so much in England is no longer there, so they could never have returned to it. When we leave the place that has been our home for so long, I ought to be happy to think that someone else is enjoying and benefiting from the pleasures of living there. In truth and with total selfishness, I think I would prefer La Puce to simply disappear as we drive away.

*   *   *   *   *

I have learned another important lesson in life. When dressed as a carrot, driving a car is even more difficult than playing the spoons. After a few false starts and a collision with the woodshed, I have handed over the controls to Donella and am vegetating in the passenger seat. I dislike being a passenger unless I have been drinking, and having my arms trapped in the costume means I am unable to indicate the correct route and any passing points of interest, oncoming cars or other possible hazards. I am also extremely uncomfortable as it is a hot day, and the height of the carrot suit means I have to kneel on the seat with almost half my body out of the window. There is some pleasure in nodding gravely at drivers and seeing their reactions as we pass, but I am relieved when we park on the outskirts of the venue for the *fête de la carotte*. This year it seems the weekend celebrations have attracted an even bigger crowd than usual, and we have to walk at least a mile to the centre of town.

Créances is a small town on the west coast of the Cotentin peninsula, and is known throughout the region for its carrots. Normans, like most other French people I have met, are not particularly enthusiastic about vegetables, but are fiercely proud - also like most other French people I know - of any regional claims to singularity. In the Cotentin we claim the highest cliffs in Europe, arguably the worst weather in the country, and inarguably the biggest, reddest and most succulent carrots in all France. The fine and sandy soil of the miles of flat coastline on this side of the peninsula is an ideal breeding ground for root vegetables, and Créances is proud to be the carrot capital of the Cotentin. Other towns in our region compete to have the finest floral arrangements marking

201

their boundaries, but on the roundabout outside this town, pride of place goes to an ornate carrot mosaic.

Now, this particular weekend brings the commune's major opportunity of the year to show off their claim to fame. The early crop has just been pulled, and for the next two days Créances will abandon itself to a near-orgy of celebration and self-congratulation. During the festival, tens of thousands of people will throng the streets and marvel at the wealth and variety of uses for the town's signature vegetable. At dozens of stalls lining the square, visitors will be able to sample and buy carrot-flavoured cake, bread, terrine, soup, wine and calvados. At some stalls they will even be able to buy carrots in their natural state.

Many artists and craftsmen will have taken on the challenge of working with the most common local material, and there will be sometimes breathtaking examples of their arts and skills. There will be intricately carved miniature sculptures of birds, animals and buildings, and minutely detailed representations of historical characters and events. Last year, the visitors marvelled at a complete representation of the storming of the Bastille crafted entirely from carrots. At other times I have seen chess sets and small items of jewellery fashioned from the town's premier product. One year there was even an attempt to hold a fashion parade of *haute couture* clothing made entirely from carrot peelings, but it was not a success. The *fête de la carotte* at Créances is also, of course, as good a reason as any to drink and eat too much over a summer weekend, so the bars and restaurants in the town will be doing very good business.

We have reached the market square, and I have become almost anonymous. It is a tradition that all the traders at the fair mark the occasion by wearing carrot colours or favours, and red hats, scarves, rosettes and complete ensembles are common. But I am pleased to note that nobody else seems to have copied my carrot suit as I battle my way through the crowd to report for duty.

At the *épicerie anglaise* stall I find our friends Sally and Alan Offord struggling to cope with the demand for their carrot fudge. Like us, they made a marked change to their lives more than a decade ago, and also like us, they are very happy to have done so. All over Britain, legions of middle-class executives spend long hours standing on crowded trains or sitting in traffic jams while dreaming of escaping to another life and world, but few will ever actually commit themselves to a real and radical bid for freedom. In their past lives, Alan and Sally were high-flying marketing consultants, helping to clinch Anglo-French business deals worth millions of pounds. They were very good at what they did, but felt somehow unfulfilled. Then came the moment of epiphany when yet another sophisticated Parisian businessman took them aside and asked awkwardly if they would bring him a jar of English marmalade on their next visit. The couple had long known that, despite their protestations, many French people do admire and enjoy some traditional British grocery items.

Deciding it was time they left the rat-race to start a very different life and line of business, they moved over to Normandy and set up shop with a market stall. It was hard-going at first, but soon they had French locals as well as British expatriates amongst their regular customers. Now they supply supermarkets across France with the best of British grocery products, but like to keep their feet quite literally on the ground while maintaining a hands-on knowledge as to whether Marmite or Bovril is the flavour of the month with their French consumers.

Retreating from the fray, Sally tells me that the appointment with Captain Vasco is in an hour and hands me my sandwich board. Officially I am in Créances to help advertise the presence of the English grocery stall, but I have also arranged a meeting with a locally renowned removals specialist. When I made the mistake of broaching the subject of a DIY moving operation to Donella, she was adamant that we employ a team of skilled professionals, so I have made a compromise. Although I know of no furniture removal companies in our area, I have been told of a man who makes a living from shifting unusual and challenging objects from one place to another. Captain Vasco is said to have inherited his talent from his father, who is alleged to have been a key figure in the evacuation at Dunkirk. It is even said by some that the special gift for accomplishing difficult removal jobs is in the Vasco genes, as the current specialist's great-grandfather was allegedly responsible for shipping the Statue of Liberty to America.

When I called, his wife said he was working in Créances today, and will be supervising the movements of the most ambitious float the festival organisers have attempted. I am now sure that he is the man for our job, and am looking forward to our meeting to discuss the details of how he will tackle the particular problems at La Puce.

Anyone who can manoeuvre a fifty-foot carrot through the crowded and narrow streets of Créances today will think little of the challenge offered by our situation, and if the stories are true, he has the special abilities in his blood.

An hour later and I have returned the sandwich board and we are sitting outside a bar while we enjoy the carnival procession. It is very impressive, and also the first time that I have seen a boat run aground in the middle of a town. In a perfect demonstration of the French creative thinking process, the committee had obviously decided to embody the two main characteristics of Créances in the design of this year's float. Together with its vegetable enterprises, the town is a fishing port and the float takes the form of a fair-sized trawler which has been disguised as a carrot. Unfortunately, it is obvious that practicality has been sacrificed in the pursuit of creativity. The only access to the square from the slipway is a narrow lane between two bars, and while the tractor towing it has passed through the gap with ease, the boat has become stuck fast.

Predictably, rather than inviting ridicule or irritation at

the delay as it might in Britain, the incident has actually added to the enjoyment of the crowd. As the tractor driver attempts to free the boat, the crowd has surged forward to help with offers of advice on what he should be doing. The owners of the two bars have also seen an increased business opportunity, and are busily setting up chairs and tables around the beleaguered vessel. Before long, waiters are ferrying dishes of *moules aux carottes* to the spectators who have decided to make a meal of the event.

As I watch the spectacle, I realise I may not have found the right man to handle our removals. It appears that Captain Vasco has more alcohol in his blood than inherited transportation skills. After watching the bearded and nautical-looking driver of the tractor empty the bottle in his hand, then fall from his vehicle and become involved in a heated exchange with a baton-waving policeman, I suggested we finish our drinks and continue our journey to view the manor house on the marshes. Captain Vasco may be a *spécialiste* in his occupation, but I do not think he will be up to getting out of all the tight corners at the Mill of the Flea.

*   *   *   *   *

We are lost in the heart of the *marais* again, and for once I cannot blame the navigator.

I am still an enforced passenger as Donella has, she claims, forgotten to bring a change of clothing from my carrot suit and we have seen the same cow three times in the last hour. Following the directions of the Count of Nulléplace, we have found Sousville, the nearest village to the mini-manor house, but one country lane looks much like another in this area of the marshlands. They all seem to wind their way down to the great plain of the central Cotentin, but so far we have seen nothing which looks remotely like a *petit manoir*. When I say that the Count's directions seem faulty, my wife suggests dryly that they were meant to be followed after dark and perhaps even as the bat flies.

Having given up our latest attempt, we return to the village and wait for evidence of human life. Of all the places I have been in the world and apart from certain backwaters of the Hindu Kush area of Afghanistan, I think that rural Normandy can be one of the least populous, or at least appear to be. This is not because there are vast areas of uninhabited terrain in our region, but because many country people do not go out much. It is an old joke in other regions of France that whole towns in Normandy close for the winter, but I know of some small communes where you could spend an entire day without seeing another human being. Curiously, in its pronoun form the French word for nobody is the same as for somebody, and in some parts of our area you can see how this may have come about. We have been sitting in the square for nearly an hour, and have yet to see a single *personne*.

Eventually I hear a noise in the churchyard and heave myself out of the car. Turning a heavily buttressed corner of the square tower, I find myself standing over an open grave and looking down at the man digging it. He is busy at his work, and when I ask him if he knows of a *petit manoir* in the locality he shakes his head without looking up. I say that I believe the house was the property of the Chartier family in the old times, and that the present Henri Chartier is a personal friend of mine. At this, the man's full attention is gained. Standing up, he takes off his cap and looks up and begins giving directions before his voice trails off. I ask him to continue, then repeat his words carefully before thanking him and making my way back towards the car. Continuing to memorise his directions, I reach the corner of the church before remembering that I am still wearing my special outfit. Looking back, I see the man stumbling between the gravestones towards a gate in the far wall. I think it would be interesting to be in his local bar this evening and hear what he has to say about his encounter with a giant carrot who asked directions and claimed to be on close personal terms with the Count of Nulléplace.

*   *   *   *   *

I think we have found our new home.

Of all the truisms regarding the buying of property in France, perhaps the truest is that Britons rarely buy the type of home they set out to find. Many seem to buy the exact opposite of the type and location and price of property they think they have been looking for. I have lost count of the number of people I have heard of who went in search of a cottage and bought a farm, or looked for an isolated rural property and ended up with a townhouse. I don't know why or how this phenomenon occurs, but it does, and now it looks as if it is happening to us.

The miniature manor house is everything we have never wanted, or rather did not think we did. The asking price is also almost twice what we can afford. I have often mocked Britons who arrive in France with plans to buy a modest home and are then wooed by the seductive evidence of just how much property so little money can buy on this side of the Channel. But, having accepted all that, the aptly-named *Le Marais* is really special and I think it could even pay its own way. I have also often mocked Britons who justify buying a big home in France by claiming they can make extra money from letting out all the rooms they will never need, but in this case it makes sense. And the place itself is a gem. Apart from anything else, *Le Marais* combines the practicality and homespun attractions of a farm with the history, grace and quirky appeal of a miniature stately home. As we both agree after our long search around the peninsula, it is pretty near perfect.

At the end of a narrow but well-metalled lane, the

impressive stone house sits along one side of a gravelled yard which is also bounded by a stable block and a barn at least as big and well-maintained as our mill cottage. Facing the stables and stretching beyond the barn is an acre of beautifully landscaped garden. Dotted around the immaculate lawn are ornamental and fruit trees, and a central rockery of granite boulders dressed with a profusion of alpine plants and spreading juniper. The magnolia tree beside the rockery has long shed its blooms, but the large yet delicate pink-veined flowers must look magnificent at their peak in April and May. At the end of the stable block is a chicken run and coop which makes our accommodations at La Puce look like slum housing. And around the corner there is more. Much, much more.

The stone balcony to the back of house overlooks at least two acres of neatly-trimmed grass surrounding a large pond and another rockery of giant stones down which a cascade of spring water bubbles. A line of tall pine trees marks the boundaries on either side of the property, and beyond a white post and rail fence lies the *marais*. At this time of year the great plain is not in flood, and appears as a seemingly limitless expanse of lush green veined with dozens of meandering tributaries and straight, narrow canals. Drawing on them as it makes the final stage of its journey across the plain and to the coast beyond is the majestic River Douve. At least three miles from where we stand, the roofs and windows of the nearest town sparkle in the afternoon sun, and a train speeds silently on its journey to Paris. Along the canals, tiny punts bob at their moorings and a vast army of tall and slender reeds moves gently in the breeze. High above, ducks and egrets and seagulls swoop and wheel, and a dozen horses make their desultory way to investigate the promise of a pick-up truck bouncing towards their feeding troughs. It is so quiet that I can hear my wife breathing, and like me, she is breathing quickly with sheer excitement at the beauty of the panorama.

Inside, the big house is almost as breathtaking as its

surroundings. Used as we are to the cramped quarters of the mill cottage, it seems that the current owners of *Le Marais* have had to think hard about how to put to use so many rooms, and been almost cavalier with the huge amount of space. Between the stable block and the house is a window-walled room which serves no other purpose than to take in the sun and the spectacular view across the marshlands. Beyond that is a spacious area which we first take to be the kitchen, but discover is merely a pantry. This leads on to a high-ceilinged and tiled-floor dining room with an oaken staircase in one corner, and beyond that lies the huge kitchen. The gleaming ultra-modern cooker, dishwasher, cabinets and work surfaces make a striking contrast to the biggest fireplace I have seen in anything less than a castle, and the blackened back wall and rows of traditional cooking implements hanging from the mantle show it is not just for show. A door from the kitchen opens on to a small lobby and another staircase leading to what must once have been the servants quarters. From the lobby, other doors lead to a cloakroom and toilet, a utility room, and a downstairs bedroom which is almost as big as the ground floor of the mill cottage at La Puce. Just when I think we have seen all the ground floor has to offer, Donella discovers a wallpaper-panelled door which leads to a shower room, complete with bidet and even a twin set of wash basins.

If we thought that the downstairs of the house had room and rooms to spare for our needs, the upper reaches of the building give us even more reason to catch our breath. At the top of the winding staircase from the lobby are three more bedrooms and a bathroom with a set of stairs leading up to a loft which could hold at least four more. Finally, beyond the bedrooms, through a paneled door and down two steps is the *pièce de résistance*. With so much space in which to let their imaginations roam, the owners have sacrificed at least three of the upper rooms to make one. All the ceilings and the attic flooring in this part of the house have been removed to reveal the rough-hewn roof supports, and the space above our heads ends only with the giant ridge beam. At one end of the huge room is a raised dining area, and at the other a fireplace even bigger than the one below. Alongside the fireplace, a door leads on to the balcony and its endless views of the marshlands beyond.

In its location and with what has been done to it, *Le Marais* is nothing short of ideal for a writer and his wife, and especially for a writer and his wife who are always in need of some additional income. In our situation, I think we may have made a big mistake just by looking at what we cannot afford. After more than ten years of writing books warning of the pitfalls on the road to finding a home in France, it seems I have fallen headlong into the most common of them all.

*   *   *   *   *

We come to the end of our tour and are recovering our breath back in the sun room. Our guides have brewed a pot of English tea in our honour, but the apple pastries are very definitely Norman. After several false starts, I manage to do them full justice by tearing armholes in the now badly wilting carrot suit which I note the vendors have been too polite to mention.

As I should have suspected from what has been done at *Le Marais*, Georges tells me he is a designer, and has spent ten years restoring the ancient house. His wife, he says, is Mad. I consider making a joke about her being crazy to even think about leaving such a place, but decide it will not translate well. It also seems a little presumptuous to question someone else's sanity while you are dressed as a carrot.

Our hosts are of around our age, and as Georges says, the stones above the graves of his ancestors are some of the oldest in the local cemetery. As we talk, it is clear that he is not as anxious as his wife is to leave the home he has just finished painstakingly restoring. Apart from all his family roots and connections binding him to this area, Georges says he is a keen *chasseur* and there is no finer hunting ground than the *marais*. But Madeleine wishes to live closer to her relatives and the town. She loves the house, but finds the sometimes brooding vastness of the marshlands oppressive. In the summer she likes to tend the garden, but in the winter she often wishes that the lights of the distant town of Chef-du-Pont were much closer. If we buy *Le Marais*, Georges says as he walks us to the gate, he would like to keep the several hectares and their lakes and orchards he owns on the other side of the lane. That way, he feels he will not have lost his connections with the area completely. If we can come to an arrangement on this piece of land, he will be able to visit and tend it at weekends, and use the old hut there as a base for his hunting expeditions while Mad remains in the townhouse she wishes them to buy. We would, of course, be welcome to use the lakes and land at any time, and he could perhaps help me with work around the house and its gardens.

I shake his hand and say that I think I understand how he must feel and what a sacrifice he is making. If we were to buy their home, I would be more than pleased for him to keep the extra land. I would also be honoured if he would be my guide to the area and its special places and people. As it is, I have to be honest and say that his enchanting home is far too rich for our blood. Georges gives the classic gallic shift of the shoulders which signifies polite rebuttal, and says that there are always ways around these things if someone wants something badly enough.

I agree, and as we wave goodbye and I take up my position half in and half out of the car, I think of what he has said and suggest to my wife that we find the nearest bar so I may ply her with drinks and come up with all the good reasons we should make *Le Marais* our new home.

*   *   *   *   *

211

We have found another minor but persuasive reason for finding some way to raise the money to buy *Le Marais*. It is little more than a mile from the house to an absolute gem of a rural bar.

Hidden behind the church at Sousville, the business is disguised as a house. The building has no plate glass window showing provisions on sale, nor any name sign or advertising hoarding. There is not even the most basic *pissoir* for the male clientele. In virtually all other remaining examples of the rural *bar-épicerie* in our area, the owner lives above the shop; at Sousville, the owner clearly prefers to be in even closer contact with her business. On one side of the central door is the grocery department, which is also the living room to the house. A few shelves of basic provisions line the walls, but the sideboard, dining table and chairs take pride of place. At the other end of the building is the proprietor's front room, in which customers are obviously allowed to take their ease and drinks. Through the window I see that the floor is carpeted rather than tiled, and the neat row of wellington boots outside the entry door signals what must be a basic rule of the house. Shrugging off our boots, we enter and find we have travelled in time. The bar at Sousville is a perfect replica of the best room in millions of small houses in France more than three decades ago. In fact, I realise, this is not a replica, but the real thing. Times have changed even in rural Normandy, but not in Madame's front room. In one corner there are two plump armchairs dressed with crisp lace antimacassars and arm covers, and a faux-bamboo table stands before them. Alongside is a sugar-twist standard lamp in apple wood topped with a large, tasselled shade. A highly-polished upright piano stands against one wall, and its lace-bedecked top bears a dozen framed family photographs. On the wall above the piano is a shelf with ornamental brackets, and on that is a model of the Eiffel Tower in cast iron and an aged bakelite radio. The far wall is dominated by a large portrait of General de Gaulle at his haughtiest, and the sides are draped with black crepe. This

212

is obviously not a house in which to acclaim the benefits of a left-wing socialist government.

I have been too busy taking in the room to notice the other customers, and become aware of three men sitting on a bench in front of a low table and beneath a serving-hatch through which pleasantries, orders and drinks are presumably exchanged with the proprietor. Having seen through the hatchway that Madame is engaged at the stove in the kitchen beyond, I incline my head as best I may, and they return the courtesy in sombre and exact unison. One of the men is the gravedigger I encountered a few hours before, which explains why his friends seem unsurprised by my choice of dress. They return to their business of staring reflectively at the portrait of the General, and I order our drinks after apologising to Madame for disturbing her at her work. Though considerably older, she is not unlike our own Madame Ghislaine in stature. She is also possibly of similar temperament, as she replies quite sharply that serving drinks is her work while the cooking is for pleasure. The aroma is delicious, and when I ask her what she is having for dinner, she asks me if we would like some. It is only a simple *cassoulet*, but there is plenty to go round if we have not yet eaten. I thank her and return to the armchairs and the task of persuading my wife that we have found our new home.

*　　　*　　　*　　　*　　　*

The bean stew has come and gone and was as rich and satisfying as the bouquet promised, and we are on our second bottle of wine. While we have been eating and before moving on to the subject of *Le Marais* and whether we can afford to even think about buying it, I have become absorbed by the mutual mannerisms of our fellow customers.

Each member of the trio seems to be of approximately the same pre-war vintage, but each is markedly different in size and appearance. The man at one end of the bench is large and heavily built and wears an old three-piece suit with the remaining buttons on his waistcoat straining to restrict his giant paunch. On his massive head he wears a small and decidedly incongruous pork-pie hat. Like his friends, he is shoeless, and sports a much-darned pair of rainbow-hued socks. In the middle of the trio is my grave-digging acquaintance, who is dressed in his workaday outfit of mud-stained brown overalls. He is slight in build, sock-less and his headgear is the ubiquitous artisan's cloth cap. As he flexes his feet, I notice his toenails are the colour of Normandy butter and long and sharply curved like the talons of an elderly buzzard. The third member of the group is tall and thin with a long, scrawny neck. He is wearing a beret and a collarless and faded black shirt, with his grey trousers held up by broad braces. I inspect his footwear arrangements and notice that one skinny toe pokes through a hole in his off-white socks.

Despite their dissimilar appearances, the three companions have obviously spent so much time in the bar together that they have become creatures of habitude. Lined up on the low table in front of them is a tumbler of *pastis*, a glass of wine and a mug of beer. In the ashtray in the exact centre of the table lay three smouldering cigarettes. As I pretend not to stare and at no given signal I can detect, the three men lean forward, pick up their cigarettes, take a draw, then put them back in the ashtray. After a moment's pause as they exhale almost identical spirals of smoke, the three lean forward again, pick up their respective glasses and take a drink. Then they lean forward and replace the glasses in exactly the same spot and at exactly the same time. I see that the man with the *pastis* has drunk slightly less from his glass than the man drinking the wine. He in turn has taken less of a draught than the man with the beer glass, so I conclude that they are even co-ordinating their consumption rate so that each glass will become empty at the same time.

I drag my attention away from the synchronised drinking and smoking team of Sousville, and turn to the task of convincing Donella of the virtues of the house and grounds we have just inspected. As I pour her another glass of her favourite wine and before I launch into my carefully rehearsed sales pitch, my wife says she knows exactly what I am going to say. Before I say it, she would like to remind me that, although *Le Marais* could never replace La Puce in her heart, it is a wonderful place and she thinks that she could be very happy there. The ultimate test of any house for sale, as I know, is to try and picture yourself living in it. She had tried the test and it had been very positive. What particularly attracted her was the superbly spacious accommodation at *Le Marais*.

I begin to say we will be able to use the spare rooms to make money, but she interrupts to say that she was thinking of the accommodation for our chickens. The pond with its running water supply would also be a perfect home for our frogs, cray and goldfish; and Hen would obviously be able to make friends with the wild ducks we saw flying above the *marais*. Milly would enjoy the freedom to roam the grounds, and in the summertime have unrestricted access to the thousands of acres beyond with no danger from traffic. In time, we would find a new cat, and she could think of no finer hunting ground for it than the marshlands. As well as thinking about the benefits to our animals, she has given some thought to what could be done at *Le Marais* to make it pay its way.

For relatively little cost, the small barn could be converted into a very attractive two-bedroomed *gîte*. To remind us of the home we have left behind, it could be called the Little Flea. Part of the stable block could be converted into a bathroom and four bedrooms, each with a french window leading out on to the grounds facing the *marais*. If the sun room became a lounge and the utility room next to it were equipped as a kitchen, this would make another complete gîte. Naturally, its name would be the Big Flea. This would leave us the whole of the main house for ourselves. Until we converted the loft into further bedrooms, I could use it as a study. In the summer, we could let out all three of the upstairs bedrooms to visiting cyclists, ramblers and other tourists exploring the marshlands. If we became really busy, we could sleep in the loft and let out the master bedroom. This left the great room overlooking the *marais*. In summer it could be used by our bed and breakfast visitors, and through the winter it would be ideal as a study and discussion room for guests on activity and hobby holidays. We could set up and stage courses for amateur painters and those interested in learning more about colloquial French. I could host a course for anyone not interested in making money from creative writing, and we could adapt my idea of inviting our readers to come and stay with us as paying guests. I might not like being the centre of their attention for weeks on end, but would have to put up with it if I wanted to live at the big house, which would of course be renamed The Marsh Flea.

As I open my mouth to comment, Donella holds up her hand for silence and continues. As I will already have calculated, the asking price of *Le Marais* is more than the total we shall be getting for the sale of La Puce even if we have to pay no capital gains tax. Then there is the cost of publishing the new book and paying off our old overdraft. There would also be the considerable expense of converting the barn and stable block to self-catering accommodation. She had done some rough mental calculations while I had been staring at the three men on the bench, and worked out what we would need to borrow from the bank if we were to achieve all our objectives. The sum might sound daunting, but if we approached the bank with a proper business plan and offer them *Le Marais* as security, she believes they will lend us the extra money. If they are amenable and we go ahead with the purchase of *Le Marais*, it will mean some hard work in the future. But we shall have a new home, and one that we can afford to live in. One day, my writing will be recognised and we will not have to worry about letting rooms to make a living. But we have no private pension scheme, and until I become well-known it would be nice to be able to pay our way through life. Finally, though it will break our hearts to leave La Puce, moving to somewhere like *Le Marais* and concentrating on its potential will soften the blow. Can I imagine the alternative, and how we would feel to wake up each morning in a small and tidy and very boring house with a neat and soulless garden?

After opening and closing my mouth and looking blankly at her for a moment, I hug my wife as best I can given the strictures of the carrot suit, ask the Sousville synchronised drinking team if they would care to bend their elbows in time with ours, and call for another bottle of wine. Sometimes I think I do not give my wife enough credit for her business acumen and imagination, and perhaps I should think about asking her to do more of the conceptualising and planning and even execution of my money-making schemes.

All is impermanence.

The last words of the Great Buddha.

August

Although we are in high summer, it seemed there had been an overnight frost as I arrived in the water meadow this morning. When I drew closer, it was as if a monstrous spider had been at work. Long skeins of gossamer thread stretched across the grass to the oaks at the far end of the meadow, and the droplets of dew sparkled like perfectly cut and polished gemstones in the morning sun.

The stunning tableau soon evaporated, as has my enthusiasm for Donella's plan to borrow a huge amount of money so that we can buy and convert the house at Sousville. Now that the time to leave La Puce draws near and we must make a decision about *Le Marais*, I am full of fear and doubt. Although I like to affect a sometimes casual attitude to money, the thought of increasing our debts rather than settling them has kept me awake at night for the last week. In our long years together, my wife and I have always managed to survive and turned our hands to anything which would keep us afloat until my writing began to pay off. But I have always thought small. We have pickled and sold onions, repaired old clothing, and sat into the small hours stuffing, licking and sealing tens of thousands of envelopes at a penny a time. I have always been a dreamer rather than a doer, and never had the courage to risk all and take on a significant challenge. When we saw the big house at Sousville, I had expected Donella to reject my idea that we should try and find a way to buy it. But in the bar that evening, she called my bluff. I know in my heart that what she has proposed makes sense, but I am still afraid. We have an appointment to see our bank manager tomorrow, and though I would not admit it to my wife I am almost hoping he will turn our proposals down. Then we will have to find and settle for a much more modest property, but will at last be out of debt for the first time since we have been together.

Tuesday 3rd:

Another day, and another tax to inflict on anyone who dares to sell their home in France. Mr Remuen called this morning to say that there is a new law he had forgotten to tell us about. Although he will calculate the final tally of what we will owe to the government, his figures must be checked and confirmed by a department in Paris which has been set up for this purpose. For their services, we will have to pay a fee of three-quarters of one per cent of the selling price of La Puce. When I ask the question, Mr Remuen gives a dry laugh and the predictable answer that the fee will not be refunded if his sums are proved to be right; nor is it likely that they will decide his reckoning is too high and that we have been charged too much. Our real *problème* will be if the estimator's assessment of how much we have spent in restoring La Puce does not arrive in time for Mr Remuen to send it off to Paris with the rest of the paperwork. In that case, we shall be liable for the full capital gains tax without any allowances for all the money we have spent over the years. He has persuaded the estimator to find time to visit La Puce at the end of next week, and all being well, the assessment will be ready before the deadline.

As we make our goodbyes, I ask Mr Remuen if he thinks there are any other new laws regarding property exchange in the pipeline. He laughs again and says he is not aware of any, but reminds me that in the Russia of Peter The Great's time there was a special tax on beards. If he hears any rumours that this is likely to be applied to property sellers in France, he will call in good time for me to have a very close shave before the completion date. He also advises me not to eat any English baked beans before coming to his office on the big day, as I will know about the rumour that there will soon be a tax on farting. After hanging up, I reflect bitterly on the French government's creative approach to maximising revenue, and how much its executors seem to enjoy a joke when it is at other people's expense.

*   *   *   *   *

We are sitting in front of our not-so-friendly bank manager as he goes through our business plan for buying and converting *Le Marais* into a home with income. Actually, he is going through Donella's business plan, as she refused to let me make any contribution to the project. For the past hour, my wife has done all the talking as she outlined our proposals and I have done little more than nod in agreement and smile encouragingly.

As I idly watch the bald spot on the top of his head, Mr Connarde goes slowly through the folder, pausing every now and then to run his finger along a line of figures or make a note on the pad beside him. As he reads he gives the occasional grunt, which sounds to me like a combination of bemusement and incredulity. Finally, he looks up and smiles like a hanging judge with a busy day ahead. He is a very thin man in late middle-age with pointed ears and sharp features, and has the overall appearance of someone who takes little pleasure in anything that life has to offer except the opportunity to pass on bad news. I smile back at him like a hopeless entrant in a beauty contest, and he adjusts the glasses on the end of his beaky nose. Then he carefully shuts the folder and hands it pointedly back to my wife. After a long period of inspecting a single fingernail, he puts his head to one side and regards Donella as if she were a horse he was considering backing.

Finally, he snaps his head back upright and nods. He is, he says, broadly in favour of our proposal. In principle, the bank will lend us the extra money we will need to buy *Le Marais* and make the conversion. The loan will of course depend on our selling La Puce and receiving the full amount so that the overdraft can be cleared, while leaving sufficient funds to pay our share towards the purchase price of *Le Marais*. The rate of interest and repayment schedule will need to be discussed and determined, and the bank will obviously require the deeds of our new home to keep in their safe possession. He will set things in motion, and we shall meet again next week to sign the necessary documents. Then, the money will be credited to our account. But only, of course, after La Puce has been sold.

We have left Mr Connarde waiting in his lair for his next victim, and I do not know whether to be jubilant or downcast. My wife has pulled it off, and if all goes well in the next fortnight we shall become the new owners of *Le Marais*. We shall also be in hock to the bank for approximately three times the amount we owed them before starting to look for a new home.

Wednesday 4th:

We have returned to the marshlands, and I am much more enthusiastic about the prospect of us making a go of Donella's plans. On the way to tell Georges and Mad our news, we have been talking about our meeting at the bank and why we each think Mr Connarde agreed to the loan. I said it is all very suspicious, as the man who has been dunning us for our overdraft for months is now willing to lend us a much greater amount. He obviously feels thwarted because we stopped him repossessing the Mill of the Flea by selling it, and now wants to see us fail with the Marsh Flea. He really thinks we will make a complete mess of our scheme, and now we are even more entangled in his web he can pounce like a spider at his leisure.

My wife gave another of the intolerant snorts of which she is becoming increasingly fond, and accused me of over-dramatising the situation as usual. We had to look at it from our bank's point of view, and especially what was in it for Mr Connarde. Before, we had an overdraft which was growing steadily with no sign of us redeeming it. Now we would have an official loan. If our plans work, the bank will get hefty interest on the money for at least the next ten years. If we fail, they have the house as security. We will only be borrowing around a third of the value of *Le Marais*, and as long as she oversees it, whatever conversion work we do will add to that value. Donella does not think that even Mr Connarde really wants us to fail, but if we do, he will be in the clear. If we succeed, he will get the credit for making a good business decision.

Whatever he thinks or wants, it is now up to us to show Mr Connarde and his bank that we are not a pair of woolly-minded dreamers with no business sense or ability. Or at least, that one of us knows that two and two make four.

While I think about what my wife has said and what it implies about her view of me, a dog-fox breaks cover and streaks across the road ahead. A large tortoiseshell cat is close on its heels. As Donella brakes sharply, my heart lurches. It is not just the shock of the sudden stop , but that the cat looks so like Cato. We look at each other and smile at our unspoken thoughts and memories, then continue our journey. As the chimney pots of *Le Marais* appear above the winding hedgerow,

Donella remarks that we have now seen it all. It was so lovely to see a cat playing a chasing game with a fox on a beautiful summer's day. I agree, but do not think the unlikely pairing was an example of friends at play. From the way the fox was bolting, I think it was fear and not fun that was the spur. Knowing my wife's animal magnetism, and unless the rumours about the strange goings-on in this part of the peninsula are true and we have just seen a phantom of our old cat, I suspect a new applicant to join our extended family may appear shortly after we take up residence in the Marsh Flea.

We have arrived at *Le Marais* and find the house apparently under siege. At least a dozen cars are lined up on the verge outside the gate, and double that number of men are crouching behind the wall or milling about in the lane. All appear armed to the teeth. They are making more noise than a stag party at the end of its run, and some of the figures seem to be aiming their guns at each other. As we pull up, I see by their clothing and armaments that we have not happened on the outbreak of a gang or civil war, but on a hunting party in full hue and cry. The men pointing their shotguns at each other are arguing about which way the quarry went, and the men crouching by the wall are the sensible ones who want to keep out of the line of fire.

I advise Donella to stay in the car, then open the passenger door and roll out on to the verge and throw myself over the low wall and into the courtyard. Though my wife may accuse me of being overly dramatic, I know that the number of innocent bystanders killed or maimed by hunters in France each year is only marginally exceeded by casualties amongst the shootists. I crawl painfully across the gravelled yard and arrive at the door to the kitchen, which opens to reveal Georges. He too is armed for battle, and as I get to my feet I am tempted to put my hands in the air. He ushers me in by pointing the gun barrel first at my chest and then at the doorway, and I gingerly squeeze by. Inside, Mad is making

224

coffee and sandwiches for the hunting party, and adds to my feelings of vulnerability by cheerily waving a large carving knife as a greeting. I am invited to sit at the breakfast bar, and Georges explains that a fox has been spotted in the corn field along the lane. I explain that we have seen it, and it is now long gone. I add that it was being chased by a cat, and he gives me the look that country people reserve for those who have lived most of their lives in an urban environment. While obviously struggling not to sound scornful, he says that this is impossible as a fox would never be in fear of a cat. Indeed, they regularly kill and eat them. I nod appreciatively and raise my eyebrows as if I have learned something new. I also resist the temptation to tell him that, while I may be a relative newcomer to the Norman countryside, I know a thing or two about the ferocity levels of feral cats and have the scars to prove it.

*   *   *   *   *

The Sousville hunting club meeting has disbanded, and it is safe to walk the streets again. I have given Donella the all-clear, and Georges is taking us on a tour of inspection of his property on the other side of the lane alongside *Le Marais*. Before they left to gather at the bar and tell each other tall stories about all the other wild animals they have not bagged, the members of the club were introduced to me as the possible new owner of Georges' house. They seemed friendly enough in spite of their obvious frustration, and I think we will be accepted into the community as long as I pretend to be interested in blood sports and Donella can be persuaded not to broadcast her feelings. That will be difficult as this part of the peninsula manages to sustain more wildlife than the population can kill, so hunting is even more popular here than in other more barren areas. According to Georges, there are just under two hundred residents in the commune, and more than one hundred and fifty of them are active members in the local association. With the normal ratio of genders and ages this means that as well as every male adult, most of the wives, daughters, grandparents and even toddlers must be enthusiastic bearers of arms. Before we leave, Georges shows us a photograph of a recent club outing, and I glare at Donella to make sure she does not alienate the person whose home we are hoping to buy. The picture is of our host and three friends sitting proudly amongst the carcasses of six wild boars which are dangling by their back hooves from a horizontal pole. The animals understandably look as glum as the men are triumphant, and the picture captures the primeval relationship between hunter and hunted which still thrives in our civilised world. To be fair and although I find the photograph somehow depressing, there is nothing that I like better than the crackling from the cheek of a young and wild pig. As Jacques Délabré says, if you want to eat a fellow creature, you must accept that it has to be killed even if you do not want to do the dirty work yourself. As I say, I do not mind the dirty work being done, but am saddened when I see human beings enjoying it.

*   *   *   *   *

Our visit to Georges' private pastures is complete, and I can see exactly why he wants to keep them to himself. Through a rickety gate and alongside a track stands a giant corrugated-iron shed which is obviously his retreat from the world, and possibly sometimes from his wife. Inside is a collection of tools, artefacts and weapons that would make a collector of rustic memorabilia go weak at the knees. Standing in a corner is a vintage punt gun, the muzzle of which nearly reaches the high roof, and alongside it a jumble of animal traps of various designs, and savage capabilities. The surprisingly fragile-looking punt which bears the massive gun stands on a pair of carpenter's horses, and a rack of traditional bamboo fishing poles is fixed to a glass-fronted cabinet containing all the accessories needed to entice and catch every sort of fish that could possibly frequent the local waters. In another cabinet is an array of shotguns, ranging in gauge and period from a beautifully engraved and double-hammered fowling piece to a shiny new pump-action model. Neatly arranged on the wall above the workbench are rows of craftsman's tools, some of which are clearly from the same era as the house across the lane.

After showing us around what he modestly calls his *petite hutte*, Georges took us round a parcel of land to which he has obviously devoted as much time and work as he has to the restoration of *Le Marais*. There are a series of artificial ponds fed by a passing canal, a virtual plantation of apple and other fruit trees, and what seemed miles of shrubs and plants in various stages of development planted in regimental rows. At the end of our circular tour, he invited us to inspect what looked like a small cottage sitting comfortably at the top of a giant oak tree. Climbing the rope ladder, we found a well-appointed hide looking out over the *marais*, complete with a brace of comfortable armchairs, a dining table and chairs and a gas cooker. In one corner was another glazed cabinet, containing books on wildlife, philosophy, biographies of France's most famous sons and a complete range of *cordon bleu* cookery recipes.

When I complimented him on the fixtures and furnishings, Georges smiled and said that just because one liked being in the countryside, there was no reason to act and live like a peasant or an animal. By now, I had realised that as well as an accomplished designer and restorer of old property, Georges is also a knowledgeable and enthusiastic horticulturist, gourmet, collector, hunter and breeder. If we do buy his home, I shall be more than happy for him to keep his feet on the ground across the lane. I think that I can learn much from this man of so many parts.

Another result of our tour is that, in spite of my time in

the most rural area of Lower Normandy, I have once again been bemused and perplexed by the contradictions in the character and attitude of the typical countryman. While we took coffee in his shed, Georges showed me what looked like the object ball in a game of *pétanque* and explained that it was the business end of the special type of cartridge used when on the track of wild boar. The hundreds of tiny balls in a standard shotgun round would merely bounce off the dense hide of a fully-grown *sanglier* even at point-blank range, but this single ball would easily penetrate the inches of tough skin, fat and tissue and rupture the vital organs. A really good shot between the eyes would stop a charging boar dead, which was just as well if you stood between it and its prospect of living another day. Ten minutes earlier, we had been watching the same man cuddling a three-day-old duckling to his breast. When I asked if he had bred the dozens of juveniles in the enclosure for shooting and then the table, he looked at me as if I had enquired whether he liked eating children. These birds, he explained patiently, were *his* ducks, not game ducks. When mature, they would take wing and fly and sport with their wild relations high above the *marais*. But they would always come home if the food containers by their pond were kept full. When I said that his birds would surely be in danger from other hunters, he explained even more patiently that this could never happen. Everyone in the area with a gun knew which were his ducks, and which were wild and thus fair game.

*   *   *   *   *

There is even more to Georges and his marshland domain.

After returning to the house, he suggested that his wife took my wife on an inspection tour of the workings of the kitchen equipment, boiler, central heating system, water pumps, fuse box and all the other things that women understood and maintained. We men, if I was interested, would take a drive out to see his *gabion*. Without knowing whether this was local *patois* for a friend from a former colony of France or a euphemism for his mistress, I agreed, and moments later we were driving deep into the heart of the *marais*.

As we bumped across a plain that will be under a metre of water when the rainy season returns, Georges warned me not to try and navigate the marshlands on my own at any time of year. He and the local people were familiar with the ancient pack and wagon trails that zigzag through the marshes, but to go off the track in even the dryest months was to risk disaster. Quicksand was bad enough, but many apparently innocent patches of reed-grass disguised bottomless pits of ooze from which there was no escape for man or beast. Every year at least one cow would defy the electrically-charged wire boundaries of its grazing area and disappear beneath the *marais*. One of the villagers had vanished inexplicably just last month, and some local people were convinced that he and his car are now sitting for all eternity below the great plain. But Georges does not think this is true as the man knew the dangerous areas as well as he knew the sharp end of his wife's tongue. Besides, the butcher's widow went missing at the same time, so it is more likely that they are together in quite a different place and circumstance.

Eventually, we arrived at a lake a mile or more from the house and beside which stood a clearly man-made, grass-covered hump. On the surface of the lake at least a hundred birds bobbed serenely, and seemed curiously undisturbed by our arrival. When I explained the English expression and observed that shooting such sitting ducks would not be much sport, Georges laughed and said it would also be a pointless and wasteful exercise as they were all wooden decoys. When I had parked the car carefully on the side of the track, he led the way up the slope of the hump before pulling aside a square of turf and introducing me to his *gabion*.

If my new friend's tree hide was comfortable, his mostly underground bunker was little short of luxurious. Along one wall was a pair of bunk beds, and against another was a cooker, sink and provisions cupboard. In the centre of the room stood a well-scrubbed pine table and two chairs, and on top of yet another glass-fronted cabinet filled with books was a portable television. From the tiled floor, a short series of steps led to a padded bench facing a narrow opening looking out on to the lake.

Inviting me to take a seat at the table, Georges rummaged in the cupboard and produced a bottle of home-brew apple brandy and two glasses. Placing them between us, he sat opposite me and said we could now get down to business. When he had important things to think about, it was to his *gabion* he came. I was one of the handful of people who had visited it or even knew where it was. In the shooting season, he and a close friend would often spend days on end here, recording the passage of all varieties of birds and only shooting enough ducks to fill the pot at home. Often he would come here alone, just to sit and look out across the *marais* and think about life and why it took us where it did. Although we had only recently met, he believed that I too liked to think about these things. I would also obviously be thinking why any man would want to sell a house with which he is so clearly content. As he had said when we first met, his wife now wants to live in town, but that is not the full story. Madeleine suffers from depression because of a tragedy in her past, and it has become worse. She has taken against living at *Le Marais* and on the marshlands, and so they must leave. It will give him great sadness to go, but it is his duty. She is his wife, and more important to him than what is, after all, just a house. But it is also important to him that the right person buys their home. Although it should be none of his business, he would like to think that the new owners will appreciate what they are getting and where they will live. He has already had an offer on *Le Marais*, but the couple were from Paris. That was not their fault, but they told him that they would only be using his home as what they called a holiday cottage. They were cash buyers, but he did not really want to take their money. If I and my wife want to become the new owners and are content that he keeps the land across the lane, he would be happy to help us.

As he begins to fill the glasses, I say that I believe fate may have drawn us here to the marshlands and *Le Marais*. I explain that, like him, my wife and I are also sad to be leaving our home. But for our own reasons we too must go, and can think of nowhere better than here to start our new lives. We have been to see our bank manager, and he has agreed to lend us the money we need. To pay it back, we shall have to let other people share our new home, but I think it will be good for them to see what this part of Normandy has to offer, and why people like him are so happy to live here. Instinctively, we stand up to formally shake hands and then sit down again. Georges lifts his glass and holds it towards me. As far as he is concerned, he says, the deal is done. We touch glasses and empty them, and as he picks up the bottle he tells me of his plans for the future.

When he and Madeleine have found and settled in their new home, he intends to start work on his shed across the lane from *Le Marais*. If I have no objection, he means to turn it into a clubhouse for his fellow hunters. He will put in an upper floor and windows with views across the marshes, and is thinking about building a proper bar in the clubroom. He has heard from Henri Chartier that I enjoy drinking and talking about the things that matter in life, and he would like to invite me to become a member of the club. When I am not writing my books we could spend some time together, with him showing me more of the marshlands and the secrets they hold. If I like the idea, we can even give the clubhouse and bar a name to mark our meeting and - hopefully - friendship.

He fills our glasses again, and I reply that I am honoured by his invitation and suggestions. I am a member of another very special club at Néhou, and we could perhaps arrange exchange visits from time to time. I have also always wanted to live near a good bar, and can think of no better location for it than a few steps from my new front door. With his permission, I would like to make my first motion as a club member of the Sousville Social Club. In the circumstances, I think a very apt name for the bar would be *Les Deux Georges.*

Thursday 5th:

I am sitting alone on the bank of the big pond. Hen and Ermintrude are fishing for the slower and more unwary members of the goldfish tribe, and the frog chorus is in full voice. Although my fears and doubts about our future at *Le Marais* have disappeared since my talk with Georges in the *gabion*, they have now been replaced by a feeling akin to guilt. In the rush to find a new home and solve our problems with the sale, I have almost forgotten what is happening to us and what the frantic activity of the past month has really been all about. It is now almost certain that we shall be leaving our home of so many happy years, and I feel that I have been somehow unfaithful to our old friend by not reflecting more on what our going will mean. Unless something quite dramatic happens, in a little more than a week we shall have left La Puce. From that moment on, all that will remain of our long association with the Mill of the Flea will be what we have done here, what we leave behind, and all the memories we will take with us.

*   *   *   *   *

A busy day ahead. Now I have returned from my reflections at the big pond, we will occupy the rest of this morning packing, and the afternoon moving Hen and Ermintrude to their new home on the marshlands.

Since I struck the deal with Georges yesterday, our situation has moved on at a pace. We have agreed a price which does not include the land across the lane from the house, and the notary responsible for the Sousville area has already been charged with drawing up the initial contract. Because of the special circumstances, no completion date will be set until La Puce has been sold and the money from the sale has made its way across and back over the Channel, our overdraft settled and the loan released by the bank. Other potential *problèmes* have also been solved. If Georges and Mad had not come to the rescue, the open-ended arrangement for completion on *Le Marais* would have left us with nowhere to live immediately after the sale of La Puce. More problematical would have been where to store all our possessions, livestock and plants.

Knowing our situation, Georges has offered us the use of the stable block to store all our furniture, and invited us to stay with him and Mad until they move out and we officially take over at *Le Marais*. He has also suggested we move the chickens to his coop, and house Hen and Ermintrude in an enclosure by one of his ponds so they can become acclimatised to their new surroundings. He has even said that we can transfer the cray and goldfish and frogs to the pond at *Le Marais* at the same time. I know that the only regular residents of the pond are some large and very voracious roach, and am hoping they will be able to survive their sudden encounter with our psychotic goldfish tribe. Georges says that Donella is also welcome to ferry all her shrubs and saplings from La Puce and plant them where she wishes. She is even welcome to dig a vegetable patch in the landscaped garden and attempt to transplant her vegetable crop, though he seems as doubtful of their chances of survival as I am fearful for the life expectancy of the current residents of his pond.

Now that we know where all our possessions are going, I can go ahead with my plans for the great move and have

233

already given the exercise a codename. In tribute to the complexity and success of the D-Day landings and because our convoy will be travelling across the Cotentin rather than the English Channel, I have called our great enterprise Operation Overland. I know that taking a few loads of household and garden goods from one place on the peninsula to another hardly compares with the biggest coastal invasion and logistics exercise in history, but I hope my small *hommage* will help bring us fair weather, luck and as much success as Operation Overlord.

*   *   *   *   *

I have seen many examples of what is called animal instinct over our years at La Puce, but none more striking than what happened at the big pond this afternoon. Even if they could understand English, both Hen and Ermintrude have been well out of earshot when we have discussed the move and their part in it. They may have guessed that something was going on when they saw Donella digging up one of the giant gunnera plants that line one side of the pond. Perhaps they realised that the move was on when they watched me netting dozens of goldfish and tempting the crays to the surface with a piece of mature camembert tied to a string. Whatever tipped them off, they have both refused to come out of the water and into the carrying case that Donella had hidden behind the caravan.

We began our attempt in a very casual manner, as both birds usually rush up the bank and demand attention as soon as one of us arrives at the big pond. This afternoon, they both stayed in the water when we appeared, and actually retreated to the island when I took a handful of their favourite cracked maize from the caravan. Our next ploy was for Donella to try to talk them up the bank while I hid behind a gunnera with a fisherman's keep net I had extended by lashing a broomstick to the handle. When she saw me crawling towards the far bank, Ermintrude gave a warning honk and both birds began racing in circles around the island just out of reach of the net. After almost an hour of frustration, I stripped off, dived in and tried to wade and then swim after them. Although I am the holder of the Cottage Grove primary school record for the fastest length of the local swimming pool in 1949, they easily outdistanced me and all I achieved was a nasty gash to the knee from a submerged and broken cider bottle.

As dusk fell on the big pond, we decided to try again tomorrow and went back to our packing in the mill cottage. First, though, I set up an overnight trap based on an article I read about snaring techniques in the rainforests of Central America. Adapting to the circumstances and available materials, I have left the caravan door ajar and covered the floor with maize niblets. There is a stick propped under the hinged table, and a piece of string stretched tautly from the table to the handle of the door. If one of the birds disturbs the stick, the theory is that the table leaf will suddenly drop and pull the door shut. Donella is sceptical that my device will work yet worried that if it does, the noise and sudden incarceration will frighten the captives. I have pointed out that there are two comfortable beds in the caravan, a feast of food on the floor, and plenty of water in a washing-up bowl I have put amongst the maize. There is even a selection of books on the shelf above the table and one of them is *Animal Farm*, so the pair would have some suitable reading to while away their time of imprisonment.

If the trap does fail to work, the only other solution I can think of is to spike a dish of maize with *calva* and leave it on the island. When the alcohol has done its work I can row over and pick up the victims, and they will wake up with a serious hangover - but safely secured in their new quarters at *Le Marais*.

Friday 6th:

No luck with my plan for trapping Hen and Ermintrude, though we did have a visitor to the caravan during the night. When I arrived at the pond this morning, I found the two birds watching me warily from the island. Inside the caravan, all the maize had been eaten and all the lace curtains and soft furnishings ripped. The air was also rank with the unmistakable bouquet of fox. It will take most of a day to clean up the mess and repair the damage, but I have other things to worry about. It is now exactly a week to completion, and we are cutting things very fine indeed if we are to avoid a huge tax bill and, in the process, the loss of *Le Marais*. Mr Remuen's official estimator arrives today to take his measurements and assess every scrap of work we have done in restoring La Puce. He will then go away and make his calculations and come up with a figure which will hopefully cancel our alleged capital gains debt to France. If his estimation of what we have spent in terms of time and materials does not agree with mine, the purchase of and move to *Le Marais* will be off, and we will be out on the streets from next Friday afternoon.

*   *   *   *   *

Almost overnight, the French government has thought up another excuse to punish house sellers. Mr Remuen has called to say that, before the sale can go ahead, we must be in possession of a certificate declaring that La Puce is free of any traces of asbestos. Our notary has arranged for the specially-trained investigator to call next Monday. He will examine all our buildings for any signs of the dread substance, and his search may involve pulling up floorboards, removing roof tiles and even stripping plaster from the walls. My part of the arrangement will be to make good the damage and pay his fee.

236

Mr Pédan has been and gone, and we have been well and truly estimated. Though I have met many precise and conscientious people in my time I think Mr Pédan would take the biscuit, but only if it were of the precise dimension, shape, colour and taste to suit his requirements. A small man with a large clipboard, a row of coloured pens in the breast pocket of his jacket and a tape measure the size of a cart wheel, he refused all offers of coffee or a drink and set immediately to work. He also refused my offer of a complete list of all the materials we have bought over the years that I had made to save him the trouble of doing his job, and would not even allow me to hold the end of his tape in case I cheated. For more than four hours he went over every inch of the farmhouse and mill cottage, poking and probing and measuring and making notes on his clipboard.

Afterwards, he spent another hour asking me questions and challenging some of my more extreme claims as to the amount of hours and money we had spent on various jobs. He is obviously no fool, and could not be persuaded that I had personally deconstructed and rebuilt the 18th-century stone bridge on the mill track. Although he was not taken in by this attempt to emulate René Ribet's wheeze with his alleged re-tiling of the cottage roof, Mr Pédan did concede that we had obviously devoted much time and money to the restoration of La Puce. But he still turned down my offer of a set of my books about our life at La Puce as evidence of all the work we had done over the years.

After also declining politely a small gift of one of Donella's apple pies and a bottle of my best home-brew *calva*, he made some final notes on his clipboard and said that he would do his best to have his assessment ready before the end of the month. When I pointed out that the deadline was actually the end of next week, he winced and said he would see what he could do. As he left, I casually mentioned the figure which would cancel out our potential capital gains tax but he affected not to hear, so we will have to wait until virtually the last moment to know if we will be moving to *Le Marais* or be truly homeless by this time next week.

*   *   *   *   *

After another fruitless attempt to coax Hen and Ermintrude off the island I spent the evening catching up with my electronic correspondence.

Amongst the hundreds of new offers to make me a millionaire in a matter of months was a plea from a young couple who have found a property in the Vendée and are undecided on whether to go ahead with the purchase. Though they love the old farmhouse, their plan is to borrow the money to restore it, then sell it on and start again. Eventually and by careful buying and selling, they believe they will be able to work their way up to a large fully-restored property with no mortgage to worry about. They know from my books that I have had some experience of property exchange in France, and wonder if I have any advice for them.

I have written to say that it is up to them whether or not they put their plan into action. From my personal experience, I would say that buying a home in France and realising a dream can be a stimulating adventure, but selling one can become a nightmare. If they do go ahead, they must certainly hang on to every scrap of evidence of their work and expenditure, and at least try to keep abreast of every new law with regard to selling property in their part of France.

Monday 9th:

We have spent the weekend continuing our preparations for the move, and I can now imagine what it must have been like for the bomb-disposal teams who had to clear up after the D-Day landings. I intend taking my entire collection of sparkling wines to our new home, and it has been a very tense, delicate and dangerous operation just moving the hundreds of wire-topped bottles from the loft of the mill cottage to the terrace outside. A bottle of ten-year-old nettle champagne exploded at the start of the operation, and had it not been for my protective clothing of a sofa cushion strapped to my chest, a reinforced balaclava helmet, wicket-keeping gloves and a pair of swimming goggles, I think I could have been severely injured. As it is, the mouse family who live in the loft have lost most of their possessions, and also, tragically, a young member of the family. I put his remains in a matchbox and conducted a simple ceremony as I hid it under the floorboards, and shall not tell Donella about the first casualty of Operation Overland.

*   *   *   *   *

The asbestos man has made his inspection, and was as apparently casual in his assessment as Mr Pédan was thorough.

The man who arrived as I was breathlessly carrying the last bottle on to the terrace was dressed in a smart suit, and obviously had no intentions of soiling or even creasing it. Although I did not want him to be too enthusiastic in his search, I wanted my money's worth and was disappointed when he did not prepare for his investigations by dressing up in a full bio-hazard suit. He also refused my offer of a loan of my protective clothing, and seemed much more interested in my collection of home-made wines than finding any asbestos on the premises. When I asked if I could provide a ladder and torch, he said he would have no use for them and suggested we open and inspect one of my attempts to create wine from weeds. He said that his real passion in life was not locating dangerous building materials but the study and appreciation of fine alcoholic beverages.

For the next hour we sat in the mill cottage as he examined and sampled a selection of my best efforts, and he finally said he was most impressed that some of them were almost drinkable. After I reminded him why he had come to La Puce, he excused himself and went on a wander around the grounds. Looking out of the window, I saw him look briefly at the roof before relieving his bladder on the compost heap by the hen-houses. On his return he pronounced himself satisfied that La Puce was free of all contamination and we shook hands and exchanged the all-clear certificate for a cheque together with a bottle of blackberry and marrow wine he had particularly liked.

Tuesday 10th:

Another day nearer to our planned departure from La Puce, and another call from Mr Remuen.

Today's *petits problèmes* concern the mortgage we took out to help buy La Puce. The final payment was made several years ago, but the interest we paid over the ten-year period is allowable against tax on our alleged capital gains. Mr Remuen called to say that, although he accepts we no longer have a mortgage, under French law it will still exist somewhere in hyperspace. Accordingly, the former mortgage must be officially declared dead, which will mean a payment of several hundred euros for the work involved in laying it to rest. The other problem is that this process cannot happen until the original existence of the mortgage can be proved. Neither can he make an allowance for the interest we paid until our bank provides the details. He has been in touch with our local branch and they have been in contact with head office at St. Lô. At neither place is there any record of a mortgage having been issued on a Mill of the Flea. Unless they can find it before Thursday evening he will not be able to make the necessary allowances; the good news however, is that we will then at least not have to pay to have the phantom loan exorcised.

*   *   *   *   *

The fifth call of the day from our notaire, who began by making a joke that his invoice to me for telephone charges could soon mount up to rival our likely tax bill. Although there is still no news from our estimator, Mr Remuen said he had heard some good news from our bank manager. After an afternoon searching through the records, his staff have found the details of our mystery mortgage. The cause of the trouble, Mr Remuen says Mr Connarde said, was my abysmal pronunciation of French words when we arranged the loan. After an unsuccessful trawl through all the documents filed under *'Puce'* as in flea, the mortgage papers and record were finally found under *'Pouce'* as in thumb.

Wednesday 11th, 8pm:

Operation Overland has taken place and was, all things considered, a success. We have lost several breakable items in transit, and more than a few other more robust pieces when Coco's Land Rover hit a speed hump on the outskirts of La Haye-du-Puits.

We also lost part of the convoy when it took the wrong turning at Sousville and became temporarily marooned in the *marais*, but the treacherous quickmud pits claimed no victims today. Our steady progress also caused probably the longest

241

traffic jam on the D2 that the area has seen since the Tour de France passed our way, but René Ribet's inspired idea of borrowing the uniform and motorcycle of a friendly traffic policeman and posing as our official escort ensured we completed the journey unmolested.

All our furniture and other belongings have been stowed away in the stable block at *Le Marais*, and we are now gathered at the bar at Sousville. To thank my friends for their help and get to know the local people and regulars, I have put a large amount of euros over the bar and Madame tells me she is having her best night since the week-long celebrations following the Liberation. The offer of a free drink has had its predictable effect on the local people's normal reluctance to leave their homes on a weekday, and the party has spilled out on to the road. It is a fine evening, and Madame has put out a number of plastic tables and chairs, and virtually all the furniture from her best room. Now that the bar has been cleared for action, the only fixture remaining is the bench beneath the serving hatch where the local synchronised drinking team are still carrying on their routine like some bizarre Victorian mechanical.

Together with many of the local residents, the leading lights of the Sousville Hunting Club have turned out in full force and have thankfully left their weaponry at home. They are telling the usual tall tales and passing round photographs of past triumphs, and our secretary JayPay has already made a list of possible dates for a combined onslaught on the wildlife of the *marais*. Henri Chartier has broken his usual rule of not venturing from his home in daylight hours, and his dramatic appearance has confirmed some of my friends' suspicions about this part of the peninsula. The Count of Nulléplace has said he intends accompanying me on a visit to Néhou and a JBC meeting in the near future, and Didier Bouvier has already taken orders for at least six plastic crucifixes from the more superstitious club members. An inter-village *boules* match is taking place on the gravel path leading to the church, and such is the conviviality of the occasion that there have been no serious accusations of cheating. As well as the entire committee and several rank and file members of the JBC, I am deeply touched by the number of old friends who turned up this morning to help with the move to our new home and have stayed on for the *soirée*.

As it is a Wednesday, the Flaming Curtains at St. Sauveur is closed for the evening, and a selection of the regulars have also made the long journey to drink to our health and happiness in the future. Jean-Claude Goulot is still wearing his suit of lights, but tells me he is considering closing down his escort agency. Despite the help of his lifestyle counsellor and pole-dancing friend Kara, business has not been good, so he is thinking of going back to his old *métier*. Now that we are leaving, he plans to call at La Puce when the new owners take over and ask if they would like him to continue the project of fitting a door or window into the hole at the ruined end of the mill cottage. Continuity is important, he says, and he will otherwise miss the calls he has been making for the past eight years to assess and prepare for the job.

Other old friends at our small celebration include my professional contacts, including the patron of the *Café de Paris* at Bricquebec and virtually every other bar owner in that town. Freddo says he organised the coach party when he heard the news of our departure from La Puce, and he and his colleagues have left their wives in charge for the night. As I will realise from the black armband that he is wearing, the occasion is more of a wake than a celebration for them as they will be losing their single most valuable customer when I bury myself in the *marais*.

*   *   *   *   *

It is after midnight, and still the party continues. My float behind the bar has long since expired, but everyone is having such a good time that there has been a whip-round to fund the festivities. The local people have lodged their desire to witness René Ribet's traditional Whirling Dervish routine, and it will take at least another dozen bottles of beer before he feels in peak condition.

Although Operation Overland has gone fairly smoothly and it has been a very enjoyable evening, I am now in a sombre mood. I have come in to the churchyard and am sitting on a bench near where I had my recent encounter with the gravedigger. As the sound of revelry drifts across the still night air, I am thinking of our first Christmas at La Puce and the *soirée* in the village hall. So much has happened in our lives since then, and so many of the people we have met and befriended during our time at the Mill of the Flea are no longer able to be with us tonight. I look at the gravestones softly reflecting the light of the waning moon and think about our former mayor of Néhou, Jean Chevalier, and about Mr Maurice and our legendary encounter with his antique wardrobe and its treasure trove of sweetly flavoured yet still lethal *calva*. And, of course, I miss so badly the tales of ancient times in the Cotentin from our past chairman and allegedly though sadly not immortal Old Pierrot.

I hear the old gate creak and turn to see Coco Lecoq has come to find me. He gives me a bottle of beer, sits down and lays a massive arm across my shoulder, then says it is not good to be alone with my thoughts on a night like this. Madame Ghislaine is waiting in the bar to ceremonially hand over the pint mug with a bicycle bell on the handle to my new landlady, and I shall have to make yet another speech. He pats my knee and says he knows what I must be thinking, and that it is understandable that I should be remembering the past and all the good times. I will grieve for La Puce in the coming months and even years, but the page has turned and it is time to move on to the next chapter in the story of my life with Donella in

France. I am a writer and must know that all things must pass. Nothing lasts for ever, and as the great Buddha said on his deathbed, all is impermanence. In time, he thinks I will come to love this tiny part of my adopted country as much as I loved the place and people I am leaving. La Puce will never really go away as long as I keep it alive in my memory, and a veritable army of people have shared and will relive my time at the Mill of the Flea. Now, it is time to think of the future and all the other stories I will be able to tell the rest of the world about this unique place and its people.

I nod and look up to see Donella waiting for me by the gate. She beckons and I stand and walk towards the lights and music and what will be the beginning of a new chapter in our lives in the Cotentin.

*   *   *   *   *

We are returning to the mattress on the floor of the mill cottage, but have decided to stop off and see *Le Marais* in the moonlight. The big house is outlined against the otherwise unbroken arch of the sky above the silent plain, and without the polluting loom of light from any nearby town, the furthest stars appear as a milky sea. Apart from the occasional hoot of an owl, all is quiet. Then comes a rustle from the direction of the corn field, and we see two shadows glide stealthily across the lane and through the hedge alongside what will soon be our gate.

I am glad to see that the fox and his mate have avoided the attentions of the local shooting club and the feral cat, and gladder still that the building where our chickens are now sleeping is made of such sturdy materials.

Thursday 12th, 9am:

It is sad to see La Puce so barren. Our footsteps echo as we walk around the empty farmhouse, and almost every sign of our long time here is gone. Outside, little appears to have changed, but I already miss the strident crow of our cockiest bantam. On the big pond, Ermintrude and Hen still sit sullenly on the island, and we still have to devise a way of capturing them before we leave La Puce for the last time. As we walk into the empty mill cottage, the phone rings. Hopefully, it is Mr Remuen with good news. If he is calling to say that the sale is off, I shall not be too unhappy. Our only problem then will be moving all our possessions back to La Puce, and finding a way to pay our debts so that our furniture and belongings will not be moved out again by the bailiffs.

* * * * *

We have been on the wildest of goose chases.

The call this afternoon was from Mr Remuen, who said that he had not yet received the assessment from our estimator. If it was not in his hands by the time his office closed, he would be unable to make the final allowances against our tax bill and we would have to pay the full amount. He suggested that we call the estimator directly and ask if he had finished his work. If he had, Mr Remuen recommended that we drove to St. Lô to pick up the report and bring it to his office immediately. When we called his office, Mr Pédan's secretary said the work was almost done and would be ready in no more than an hour. We broke all records for the journey, parked in a tow-away zone and rushed in to our estimator's office. The package was waiting, and on the journey back to St. Sauveur I could not resist breaking the seal on the envelope. At the end of the five page report on his inspection of the work done at La Puce over the last thirteen years, Mr Pédan had written his official estimate of what he believed we must have spent, allowing for inflation and adding a token hourly rate for our labours. The figure was within a few hundred euros of the very unofficial estimate I had mentioned as he left La Puce last week. This meant we would have to pay the minimum capital gains tax. But only if we reached the bureau of our *notaire* before closing time.

Fifty four minutes later we screeched to a stop outside the office, but saw no sign of Mr Remuen's car. His receptionist was standing by the door, turning a key in the lock. She said that he had left an hour ago to see a client on his way home. I asked if she would re-open the office so we could leave the envelope on his desk for urgent attention in the morning, or call him on his mobile phone so that we could put it in his hands. She smiled and said that there was no need to panic, as the estimator had personally faxed a copy of the document to her boss a few minutes before we had collected it.

I slumped back against the office door, then walked wearily back to the car to suggest to my wife that we visit the Flaming Curtains for some urgent retail therapy.

*   *   *   *   *

We have spent most of what will probably be our last night at La Puce looking for our balletic goose.

When we visited the big pond for another effort to persuade the two birds to leave the island, Ermintrude was nowhere to be seen and little Hen was swimming around the pond as if looking for her friend. After searching everywhere, we had to accept that Ermintrude has left us as suddenly and inexplicably as she arrived. Though it is a blow, I said to my wife that we should try not to be too sad. Ermintrude appeared when we returned to La Puce after a long absence, and now that we are leaving for the last time she has decided to move on. Perhaps she has returned to wherever she came from. Perhaps she may come back after we have gone. We both know in our hearts that little Hen will not be coming with us to our new home, and if Ermintrude returns it will be good to think that the two friends will be together.

Friday 13th, 10.05am:

We are saying goodbye to La Puce, and have reached the ancient, tree-ringed water basin we like to call the grotto.

I am thinking about all the times we have sat here watching our little stream tumble down on its endless journey to the sea. My mother liked it here and was convinced that the millers secret hoard was buried somewhere beneath the surface of the basin. To please her I spent a whole day diving in the always-chilly waters, but found only an old boot, dozens of empty wine and beer bottles and most of a wartime motor cycle.

We move on past the hen-houses, now strangely silent. Through the archway of trees lies the water meadow, and I see that it will be a spectacular year for our flag irises.

They are the ancient symbol for this part of France, and another money-making scheme I never saw through was the idea of culling and selling them to local garden centres each year. Down the slope, and we pick our way across the low wooden bridge between the two small ponds and along the meandering path to the caravan. At the big pond, Hen is still circling the island and pauses to look at us as we sit on the upturned skiff that is now home to a family of water rats. Last night when we returned from the Flaming Curtains and in spite of Donella's agreement that we must leave our feisty little duck behind, we made one last attempt to catch her. For the first time in a week, she waddled cautiously up the bank when

248

my wife held out a handful of maize, but refused to come within arm's reach. As she turned back to the water, Donella made a despairing dive, but Hen flapped off and away. It is obviously fated that she remains here, and we shall have to remember her as she is now.

We walk on past the rickety landing stage where I set off the single rocket to welcome the new millennium, and over the tombstone bridge that René Ribet claimed he bought cheaply from the undertaker at Bricquebec because the name etched on it had been misspelt. Past the stump of the giant beech which was stolen before we moved in to La Puce and along Hunters Walk is the Hobbit Tree. In reality, it is an old and mostly hollow oak, and a favourite spot of my beloved dog Lucky. When he died, I buried him here. When we knew we were leaving La Puce, Donella asked if I would like to take Lucky with us. I said I could not face the thought of revealing the little pinewood box she made for him, but I have seen the freshly-disturbed earth at the base of the tree and know that he will be joining us at *Le Marais*.

Back along Hunters Walk to the ford and stone chute that gave La Puce its name, and into the copse where I pursued our freedom-loving and doomed duck Blanche. Now we walk past the mill cottage and over the wooden bridge, and I think of all that has happened in this small dell across the years. It seems impossible that, like all those who have gone before us, we will leave no reminder of our guardianship of La Puce other than the physical signs of our occupation. Perhaps some time in the far future someone will learn how to record what has gone before in any place and summon up the sights and sounds and emotions that I think must imbue any place where people have lived, loved and died. Till then, we will have our memories, and can only guess at the lives and times of all the generations who have preceded us at La Puce.

My thoughts are disturbed by the familiar buzz of a moped as our postman delivers his last package to the current owners of the Mill of the Flea. As he pulls up beside us, I see that Patrick has taken to wearing his official crash-helmet again. When I ask him why, he blows his cheeks out and says it would obviously be madness not to. When I ask if he is still taking his vitality potion, he gives a shrug and says that he discovered the so-called miracle medicine is nothing more than a cough linctus. As soon as he knew what it was, its effect somehow stopped working. To tell the truth, he is quite relieved that his time as a rampant stud is over. It was good while it lasted, but nice to be back to normal.

We shake hands and he says that he cannot say that he is sorry we are leaving as our absence will lighten his daily load considerably. But he wishes us well, and hopes to see us again when we come back to visit the area. I watch him ride carefully up the old mill track, then we begin to open our last delivery of mail. As I look at a circular advertising cut-price televisions, my wife gives a grunt of dry amusement and hands me the letter she has been reading. I see that it has the symbol of the European Union at the top, and that the letter is a further response to an enquiry I made some months ago. After all the unsuccessful grant applications I have sent on behalf of the Jolly Boys Club of Néhou, my request for information on possible subsidies for growing trees has borne fruit. The secretary to the relevant committee has written to say that there are several schemes to encourage the planting and nurturing of trees in certain parts of Normandy, and our fields at La Puce may well qualify for a significant grant. I smile at Donella and put the letter in the porch of the mill cottage for the attention of the new owners. They may be interested in the scheme, but for us it is too late. The page has turned and it is time for us to move on.

Almost time to go. We have completed our walk through thirteen years of memories, and I am standing by the front door of the mill cottage. I have tied the mattress to the roof of the car and filled the back with the few remaining items that will travel with us to our meeting at Mr Remuen's office and then on to our new home. That is, of course, if all goes according to plan. As it is said, nothing is over until it is over, and unexpected things have a way of happening to us.

Donella is at the big pond saying goodbye to Hen, and before I call her I pick up a rusty nail from the gravel in the turning circle. On the day we arrived at La Puce, I was fascinated by a date and initials scratched by an unknown hand into the stone lintel over the door of the mill cottage. I have often looked at the lintel and wondered about the life and story of whoever made his or her small claim to immortality on that high summer's day in 1776. Now, I take the rusty nail and add our initials and the date. It is not much of a record, but we have left our mark on La Puce in so many other ways. Because of what we have done here, we know the mill cottage and farmhouse will live on, and perhaps even for centuries to come.

My wife arrives beside me and I put my arm across her shoulders. I can see that she has been crying, but she smiles when she sees what I have done before pointing out that I have used the wrong initial for her middle name. I say that it is just about par for the course that I should make one final cock-up before we leave, and we both hug each other and laugh before we cry. I hand my wife the key to the door, but she shakes her head and goes to wait in the car with Milly. I lock up for the last time. As I look around, I see that we are in for a bumper crop of chestnuts from the tree beside the wooden bridge. Then I remember that it will not be us who will harvest them.

Before getting into the car, I look at our old home and

hope that it will treat the new owners as kindly as it has treated us across the years, and that they will be as happy here as we have been. I think it is true to say that home is where the heart is, and wherever our lives take us, a part of our hearts will always rest at La Puce and the Mill of the Flea.

Goodbye old friend, and thanks for all the golden memories.